The Wisdom of the Fourth Way

*Origins and Applications of
A Perennial Teaching*

By

Theodore J. Nottingham

ISBN 978-0-9837697-0-5

Printed in the United States of America.

Table of Contents

PREFACE

A number of contemporary spiritual masters have prophesied the emergence of previously hidden knowledge into the mainstream of society. The Teacher from Nazareth was recorded as saying: *"Whatever is hidden is meant to be disclosed."* Others foretold the distortion of their teaching as more and more persons consider themselves qualified to interpret them. At the same time, many visionaries see in this phenomenon an extraordinary hope: the spiritual evolution of the species.

THE SIGNS OF THE TIMES

In this turbulent twenty-first century, in the midst of worldwide social meltdowns, in the shadow of two world wars and astonishing technological advancement, uncontrolled population growth and environmental devastation, there is a profound restless stirring among many people. We are caught in a strangely paradoxical time. While religious institutions fade in influence, there is a tidal wave of spiritual hunger sweeping across the world. As people become enslaved consumers of electronic gadgetry, there is a growing nostalgia for the simple way of life that our forbearers experienced in the heart of nature. While the unity of the planet's inhabitants becomes ever more clear and necessary, separation and intolerance are on the rise in every country.

A new perspective is being sought in the midst of this turmoil, a new relationship with others, nature, and with the spiritual aspect of our being. There is a new sense of universal relatedness and of vistas yet untapped in the human potential. This dynamic, intuitive and holistic activity has been named "New Age" even though it is rooted in a rediscovery of ancient, perennial wisdom teachings.

Unfortunately, the term "New Age" was taken over by savvy marketers who have made a fortune in the sale of books, CD's, and a variety of brickabrack offered up as tools for personal development. Incense, metaphysical books, crystals, ancient mythology -- all these are merely surface props to something much more powerful and profound. This "something" does not belong to retailers and has no price tag associated with it. At best, the merchants provide materials that can help authentic seekers to find "it."

The confusion and chaos that is labeled "New Age" merely reflects a hunger and yearning that exists within the human soul. This need to find a connection with or an integration into a vaster dimension of life has been part of the human journey from the beginning. What makes our era a special historical period is the fact that so many people are becoming aware of this inner urge to be more than consumers chained to a dreary materialistic society that has attempted to purge mystery and wonder out of the very essence of life. Moreover, these persons are also experiencing a new sense of connectedness with the environment and with the many faces and insights of humanity around the globe.

Just as the Internet has brought us all in contact to such an extent that we can reach distant continents in a split-second, so too does this new burgeoning awareness give us access to all the varieties of humankind's wisdom concerning the meaning and purpose of our existence.

This hunger and yearning that has created a marketplace for "New Age" commodities is nothing less than an evolutionary urge for personal transformation. The shrinking of planetary and cultural distances have coincided with the need to discover a new identity, one that is not chained to nationalism, racism, or even to religious belief.

It ought to be clear to any thinking person that the very future of the species is at stake in the fostering of this evolutionary development. The monstrosities of terrorism in the name of a loving God, of "ethnic cleansing" in the Balkans and in Rwanda -- not to mention the ongoing tensions in our own society -- are proof that technology and science have not taken us to a new stage of human enlightenment. They are not the saviors they were once taken to be. Their benefits are well known, but neither a cellular phone nor a faster modem can bring us the wisdom and compassion that are signs of the maturing of the human soul.

One of the characteristics of our age is the extraordinary availability of knowledge dealing with humanity's spiritual development. From the summits of the Himalayas to the inner sanctum of ancient Christian monasteries, all the teachings that were once inaccessible, secretive, or requiring long preparation can be found at the corner bookstore. Only forty years ago, western societies were uninformed by the wisdom of other lands or even by the origins of their own dominant religion. Now there are no more excuses for resisting the injunction to "seek and you will find."

The fundamental questions that make up the signs of our time are: What are we to find? What will satisfy this inner yearning? What will put an end to confusion and despair? This is where many marketers of the "New Age" do us a profound disservice. In their attempt to attract as many customers as possible, they sometimes skew their products toward personal power or self-gratification. This is the opposite direction of the evolutionary development needed in our age. In fact, the "New Age" is a rediscovery of the "old age" teachings on the death of the superficial ego so that the vaster Self where unconditional love reigns may be uncovered.

FROM COUNTER CULTURE TO MAINSTREAM

Back in the seventies, a seeker of spiritual understanding had to dig deeply into the substrates of our society in order to uncover esoteric teachings. There were no "New Age" shelves in the local bookstores and certainly no texts of the magnitude of a teacher like G.I. Gurdjieff available at a B. Dalton's or a Waldenbooks. Seekers of serious, life-transforming knowledge often followed their instinctive thirst for the sacred utterly isolated and with few or limited road maps. The commercial world around them knew nothing of their existence and saw no value in their writings. Author Colin Wilson rightly called such persons "Outsiders".

In ages past, one had to enter the Holy of Holies of Near Eastern ziggurats, or be led into the underground chambers of the Knight Templars, or receive an invitation to discreet meetings of nineteenth century theosophists, or belong to cult-like groups bound together in secrecy.

Today, across the world, there is a massive releasing of this previously hidden knowledge. For less than a fast-food lunch, a seeker can purchase information that not so long ago would have required intensive initiation and painful sacrifice. This fact is a clue to the downside of the surfacing of esoteric teachings.

How much easier it is to feed the curious intellect than to incarnate ideas that transform behavior, attitudes, and life directions.

All around us there are ad campaigns and infomercials for metaphysical products. Though it is good to know that more people are attracted to this realm, the danger of trivialization and dilution is very great. This has been the fate of all the world religions with the result being that the teachings often turn into their opposite.

So it is with esoteric truth reduced to exoteric status. When the core of spiritual knowledge is presented indiscriminately, out of context, and even with pizzazz and fanfare, something akin to an alchemical change takes place: the lower eats the higher. The shocking saying of Christ warning us not to "throw pearls before swine" is a truism that can be easily verified. Try offering profound, paradoxical and radical teaching to someone who is unprepared or uninterested. The mysterious metaphysical law that insists on the readiness of the receiver is as obvious as magnetic or gravitational forces.

This is also the other side of the coin: there is more readiness for such knowledge and transformation! There is an awareness of the interdependence of all things, of the relationship between formerly separated fields like quantum physics and mysticism. The very darkness of our times intensifies the need for light and people are turning in droves toward the more esoteric aspects of reality that just might give them meaning, hope, and fulfillment.

Most readers are undoubtedly familiar with the saying "*when the student is ready, the master appears.*" Surely, we can recognize that the influx of materials into the marketplace is related to a powerful current of interest emerging in the hearts and minds of contemporary people. This hunger for spiritual insight and wholeness is great cause for hope in a better future.

In the midst of a soulless materialism that is sinking our civilization like a deadly weight chained to its heart, there is a mysterious and widespread groping for the divine light that can set us free.

This urgent craving, relentless yearning, or gnawing emptiness is a perfect metaphor for the magnetic attraction of spirituality. Over the last twenty-five years, this interest in spiritual evolution has caught hold of more and more seekers. In fact, the attraction itself has matured and we now find individuals discarding the colorful and enticing forms of spirituality in favor of its deeper dimensions.

Beyond all the teachers and knowledge and practices lies the discovery of the inner master whose ultimate work is our individual metamorphosis.

MERCHANDIZING THE TRUTH

Unfortunately, entrepreneurs and merchants have also discovered the esoteric. There's gold in them there mysteries! Statistics from the American Booksellers Association estimate that sales of spiritual books have gone from $573 million in 1986 to over one billion dollars in 1998, and expanding ever since with the rise and virtual take-over of ebooks and digital gadgets replacing old ways of transmitting information.

Add to this the fact that most people are traveling without a compass, with no valid tradition to offer them foundations, boundaries or even suggestions and the results can be disastrous.

There are a great deal of naive, gullible people eager to put their money down for the slightest drop of "living water." This sad state of affairs has now attracted an avalanche of second rate books and gadgets that have thrown a smoke screen over the spiritual journey. Even certain of our more respected authors are obviously cashing in on this harvest of starving souls, generating material sprinkled with more hype than truth.

We now find esoteric teachings riddled with materialistic enticements such as how to live longer and make lots of money. The dilution of powerful, life-changing ideas, compounded by a reckless synthesis of traditions and practices is producing a hybrid, polyester version of spirituality. The outcome is generally found to be a series of half-truths with many steps missing in between. For instance, the great mystic of the fourteenth-century, Meister Eckhart, can say the following: "*Your 'yours' and his 'his' ought to become one 'mine'.*" A contemporary New Age merchandizing guru might translate this idea as: "I am God." What has been left out is the whole psycho-spiritual process of self-awareness, detachment, surrender and transmutation of ego-based thoughts and feelings that might possibly lead a Meister Eckhart to make such a statement. This is where the wisdom of that still little known, and often grossly misrepresented teaching known as the Fourth Way enters the arena of modern human evolution.

Perhaps esoteric products ought to carry a warning label: There are no easy short cuts and the commitment to inner development involves a lifetime of effort.

THE DISTORTION OF PERSONAL POWER

One of the greatest dangers in the marriage between spirituality, esotericism and the marketplace is the manipulation of the very purpose of metaphysical ideas. Many consumers of bar-coded esoteric teachings are attracted by the promise of increased personal power. While it is true that self-mastery, enlightened understanding and insight into the behavior of others result in a form of empowerment, the presence of self-interest poisons the whole affair.

The esoteric is naturally a world of paradox and multiple dimensions. A saying such as "the first shall be last" is as infinite in meaning as is the soul who receives it. It is only too easy to take a slice of truth, package it with style and marketing skill, and release it to a particular audience and its particular interests.

"Know thyself" can lead to the crudest narcissism or to the discovery of our ultimate identity as "No-Self". The acquisition of control and insight also enables the skillful domination of others which is anathema to authentic spiritual awakening. This same self-interested focus is packaged in much of the "pop" psychological/spiritual materials that often cater to our less noble desires. The elixir of higher consciousness is bottled as "personal power" rather than as unconditional love.

Even with the increased number of seekers, it is probable that those who genuinely seek the annihilation of the ego-self in favor of the transcendent "Overself" (as philosopher-mystic Paul Brunton names it) will remain very small. Nevertheless, much of the spiritual hunger must be considered authentic and a good many of the metaphysical publishers, New Age store owners, and product manufacturers are involved in a ministry to humanity. Such devoted persons are in fact making our world a better place.

This is the era of small presses operating on heroic effort and a sense of mission. Gems from all parts of the world and from every conceivable religion and culture are available on virtually every corner. As might be expected, in the harvest of abundant wheat there are also plenty of tares. Yet there is reason to believe that many seekers will manage to find their way through the deluge of merchandise and be drawn toward the knowledge and teachers who are steeped in the common universal truths of compassion and surrender to the Good.

FINDING A COMPASS

The key to navigating through the treacherous waters of marketed spirituality is through the tool of discernment. This attribute is central to the spiritual journey and is developed only through the maturing of an individual devoted to the path of awakening. The mistakes, dead ends, disappointments and bruises are simply part of the process. Eventually, there comes a time when the issue is no longer whether to buy yet another book or find another mentor, but to increase our ability to manifest self-transcendent love. That is the "open sesame" to the true esoteric treasures, those that cannot be put on a shelf or advertized through mail order catalogs.

Those of us committed to the inner life and its power of transformation ought to be grateful for the many avenues now available for spiritual knowledge. The chances are increased that the right book will fall into the right hands at the right time.

Nevertheless, esotericism in this new age cannot be a business without running the risk of betraying itself. Nor can it be merely a hobby for the intellectually astute, the intuitively sensitive or the alienated rebel. Still less does it belong to a particular culture or elite group. The discovery of esoteric truth is our birthright as children of the universe. No teacher, no book, no system has the final word. Spirituality is meant to awaken the Higher Self who guides us onto a road of purpose, fulfillment and service. However it is packaged and marketed, the only true value of the product is the extent to which it leads us into the intimate depths of our own being where we can each verify, assimilate and become the truths underlying all true teachings.

PART 1

THE PRACTICES OF THE FOURTH WAY

"How can you change if you remain the same?"
Maurice Nicoll

I
GURDJIEFF:
TEACHER OF RADICAL TRANSFORMATION

The teachings of George Gurdjieff are at the core of all that is most profound in religions, philosophies, and esoteric knowledge. He presents us with practical, uncompromising self-discovery, self-realization and self-transcendence. Gurdjieff said the following about his ideas: *"This teaching is for those who are not satisfied with what they have found in life and who feel that there must be something else beside success and failure in life and beyond what they have been taught in school and by their upbringing."*

The ideas that he brought to the West and the system of work on oneself which came to be known simply as "The Work," have the power to transform human consciousness and its understanding of reality. Anyone who begins to practice for a time the efforts of self-observation, divided attention, and self-remembering under the guidance of someone who has understood and lives the teachings will discover their radical impact on the human psyche.

Gurdjieff essentially synthesized ancient esoteric teachings and made them approachable and applicable to the lives of rational Western individuals. A seeker will find in his teachings an immeasurable treasure, the essence of so many other teachings, both spiritual and psychological, on the inner life. This extraordinary system of thought, which ranges from the most intimate, psychological insights to a grandiose cosmology linking the individual with the universe, is a synthesis of practices and teachings known as The Fourth Way. It is named the Fourth Way to differentiate it from the other ways of conscious evolution: the Way of the Monk, the Way of the Fakir, the Way of the Yogi. Each of these classic methods of human transformation focus on different aspects of the individual: emotional, instinctive, intellectual.

17

The Fourth Way deals with all of these dimensions at once, seeking to create a balanced individual whose inner work of transformation occurs in the midst of his or her daily activities. There is no need for monasteries, ashrams, or physical asceticism. Yet the efforts made are as intense and demanding as any of the practices which take place in those settings. The "Work" is entirely inner, invisible, and individual.

Then there is the man himself. Gurdjieff was the archetypal Master, beaming with extraordinary psychic powers developed in secret schools and monasteries somewhere between the Caucasus and the Himalayas; brutal soul-shattering insights; marvelous humor which was both ribald in the extreme and breathtakingly penetrating. He also had a capacity for love that was matched only by his ability to express rage. He was a master hypnotist, a master actor, a master healer. Those who encountered him often had opposite ideas of who he was, usually as a result of his own intentional behavior. He sometimes gave the impression of being a simple charlatan to arrogant individuals who would come to question him, while to others he was the most enlightened man they would ever encounter.

This powerful Master with eyes that pierced to the depths of the soul was also an old man whose pockets were full of candy for the children. This mysterious outsider who revealed new horizons that tore down society's social conventions and cherished beliefs, was also closely, though secretly, associated to the Russian Orthodox community in Paris. Several important teachers in their own right were born from his tutelage. P.D. Ouspensky is the most famous one. He presented the Work from a more intellectual perspective, though it still remained very practical. His book, *In Search of the Miraculous*, is one of the best expressions of the work ideas available to us.

Other leading students included Rodney Collin and Maurice Nicoll. Both have written remarkable books that shed light on what is now called the Gurdjieff-Ouspensky work. Nicoll's *Psychological Commentaries on the Teaching of Gurdjieff and Ouspensky* consist of a five volume set of essays that cover the minute details of working on oneself. Gurdjieff called this path the way of the "Sly Man." This term is a poor translation of the French "*le ruse*" which has less negative implications and might better be translated as "clever" in transforming the difficulties of the moment into opportunities for spiritual awakening. Similar to the Zen Buddhist masters and their saying that "each moment is the best opportunity," Gurdjieff wanted his students to learn how to use the circumstances of each moment -- both the internal and external -- as food for the development of a new state of consciousness.

THE WORK

P. D. Ouspensky opens his lectures recorded in *The Psychology of Man's Possible Evolution* by stating that psychology has lost touch with its origins and its true meaning. He argues that, in its essence, psychology is the oldest science known to humankind and a largely forgotten one in spite of the fact that never before in history have there been so many psychological theories. He suggests that psychological systems can be divided into two categories:
1. Systems which study the person as they find him/her or as they imagine him/her to be (these are our modern systems).
2. Systems which study the person not from the point of view of what he/she is or what he/she seems to be, but from the point of view of what he/she may become.
These last systems alone explain the forgotten origin and meaning of psychology. According to Ouspensky, psychology is "the study of the principles, laws, and facts of man's possible evolution." His fundamental assumption is that human beings are not completed persons. Nature develops us only to a point, and it is only by individual efforts that further development proceeds. He writes: *"Evolution of man in this case*

will mean the development of certain inner qualities and features which usually remain undeveloped, and cannot develop by themselves."

The evolution of human consciousness is a question of personal efforts and is therefore a rare exception among the majority of human beings. To those who would wonder at the seeming unfairness of this assertion, Ouspensky responds that most people simply do not want to awaken. To become a different being, we must want it greatly and over many years. Without the necessary efforts we will not evolve. Moreover, we must acquire qualities which we believe we already possess but in fact do not. In the Fourth Way, this insight is the first step in the direction of inner evolution: we do not know ourselves.

The teaching tells us: "Man has invented many machines, and he knows that a complicated machine needs sometimes years of careful study before one can use it or control it. But he does not apply this knowledge to himself, although he himself is a much more complicated machine than any machine he has invented." This "machine" is brought into motion by external influences. All actions, ideas, and emotions are responses to the stimulus of external events.

For Gurdjieff and Ouspensky, such mechanical persons are asleep to their true condition and virtually incapable of change. "By himself, he is just an automaton with a certain store of memories of previous experiences, and a certain amount of reserve energy." Everything happens to us as to puppets pulled by invisible strings. Ouspensky believes that if we could perceive this phenomenon, then things would begin to change for us. We human beings are not merely stimulus-response machines, but machines which can know that we are machines! Realizing this, we may find ways to cease being simply reactive organisms.

THE ILLUSION OF UNITY

Another central idea in the Fourth Way is that the individual is not one. We have no permanent "I" or Ego. Every thought, feeling, sensation, desire is an "I" which believes that it is the whole person. Yet none of these "I's" are connected and each depends on the change of external circumstances. To make things worse, there are often impenetrable defenses between each "I" which the Work calls "buffers" separating these subpersonalities from one another.

Gurdjieff states that one of our most important mistakes we make is our illusion about our unity. He writes: "His "I" changes as quickly as his thoughts, feelings, and moods, and he makes the profound mistake in considering himself always one and the same person; in reality he is always a different person, not the one he was a moment ago." Our every thought and desire lives separately and independently from the whole. According to Gurdjieff, we are made of thousands of separate I's, often unknown to one another, and sometime mutually exclusive and hostile to each other.

The alternation of I's is controlled by accidental external influences. There is nothing in us able to control the change of I's, mainly because we do not notice it. Each separate I calls itself "I" and acts in the name of the whole person. This explains why people so often make decisions and so seldom carry them out. A little self-observation will prove that we usually think, feel, move and respond to the stimulations acting on us, without our being aware of what is happening within us. This self-observation is in fact the first practical effort required in the Fourth Way. The student is to create an "observing I" which observes with objectivity his or her inner activity. To develop an objective space within which can see without judging is extremely difficult but is also the first breakthrough out of our mechanical behavior and the virtual hypnotic trance in which it keeps us.

STATES OF CONSCIOUSNESS

Dr. Kathleen Speeth, from the California Institute of Transpersonal Psychology, has suggested that what Ouspensky and his teacher Gurdjieff have proposed are psychotherapeutic techniques which bring the various fragments of the ego into awareness, gradually acquainting the "I's" with one another. But there is another element in the Fourth Way view of human beings which creates a backdrop to the ideas just mentioned. This has to do with the very concept of consciousness.

Ouspensky dismisses the notion that consciousness is equivalent to mind activity. Consciousness is a particular kind of awareness concerning who we are, where we are in the moment, and what we know in the deepest dimension of our being. It never remains the same but can be made continuous and controllable through special efforts and study. The Fourth Way points to four states of consciousness: sleep, waking state, self-awareness, and objective consciousness. Most everyone lives only in the first two states.

The third state, self-consciousness or self-awareness, is one that we believe we possess even though we are conscious of ourselves only in rare flashes. Such flashes come in exceptional moments, in highly emotional states, in times of danger, or in new and unexpected circumstances. We have no control over their coming and going. This state of consciousness is similar to the Buddhist concept of "mindfulness" which Thich Nat Than describes as "keeping one's consciousness alive to present reality." However, the Gurdjieff teachings provide more details about our ordinary state which is described as "sleep," the same state referred to by Christ when he said "Watch! Do not sleep."

Ouspensky writes concerning this condition: "If we knew the quantity of wrong observations, wrong theories, wrong deductions and conclusions made in this state (our ordinary consciousness), we should cease to believe ourselves altogether." Dr. Speeth, in her book *The Gurdjieff Work*, observes that anyone who has a difficult time accepting the notion that as we are we have but few moments of true self-awareness, ought to make a study of the loose jaws and vacant stares of people in public places and in situations where they do not think that they are being observed.

According to the Fourth Way, the central obstacle to higher levels of consciousness is a phenomenon known as "identification." Ouspensky describes it in this manner: "In this state man has no separate awareness. He is lost in whatever he happens to be doing, feeling, thinking. Because he is lost, immersed, not present to himself, this condition is known as a state of waking sleep." When we are identified, our attention is directed outward and we are lost to ourselves. Self-awareness is then a state in which we become aware of ourselves and are no longer hypnotized by the external event before us.

There is a higher level still to be reached which the Work calls "objective consciousness." In this state, we come into contact with the real world from which we are cut off by the senses. Some psychologists deny the existence of higher states of consciousness, dismissing them as dream-states. It is strange that Sigmund Freud, who discovered so much about subconscious states, should not have postulated the existence of levels of consciousness above as well as below the level on which we usually live. But in order to reach the more silent areas of consciousness, what the Work calls our "higher centers," we must get beyond the noisy regions of our minds in which we spend so much of our time.

The attainment of higher levels of consciousness is closely related to certain religious practices which are found in all cultures, such as meditation and contemplation. These are difficult paths to tread because our attention is always being caught by the ceaseless chattering in our heads. Yet it is possible to become receptive to a state of pure consciousness without thought, a state in which truth is revealed to us directly, without the use of words.

ESSENCE AND PERSONALITY

In order to see clearly the roots of our psychological distortions, the Fourth Way defines two aspects of the individual: essence and personality. Essence is what a person is born with, personality is that which is acquired. All that is learned, both unconsciously through imitation and through acquired likes and dislikes, constitutes the outer part of the person, that which is changed by outer circumstances. Though personality is necessary, it must not be left to dominate essence or it will produce artificial persons cut off from their true natures. "This means that with a quick and early growth of personality, growth of essence can practically stop at a very early age, and as a result we see men and women externally quite grown up, but whose essence remains at the age of ten or twelve."

Through the practice of *self-remembering*, we can separate ourselves from the pretenses and imitations which have enslaved us since childhood and return to who we actually are. Such a return to our essential nature is accompanied by a sense of liberation unlike any other. "To thyself be true" is the first commandment on the way of self-development and the attaining of a higher consciousness.

According to Rodney Collin, one of Ouspensky's primary students who started his own Fourth Way School in Mexico, the fundamental abnormality in human beings lies precisely in the divergence between personality and essence. The more nearly we know ourselves for what we are, the more we approach wisdom. The more our imagination about ourselves diverges from what we actually are, the more insane we become. He writes: "Unless a man first finds himself, finds his own essential nature and destiny, and begins from them, all his efforts and achievements will be built only on the sand of personality, and at the first serious shock the whole structure will crumble, perhaps destroying him in its fall."

For Rodney Collin, the soul is the totality of the moments of self-awareness during one's life. Yet moments of higher consciousness are very rare and gone as soon as they come. Once again, the reason such self-consciousness is so difficult to attain is that it is dependent on the conscious use of attention.

SELF-REMEMBERING

One of the most practical and meticulous study of the ideas of this inner work on oneself is found in Maurice Nicoll's masterful *Psychological Commentaries*. Here the reader will come upon the "nuts and bolts" of transformation. Nicoll states somewhere in these five volumes of lectures given to his students that, as you make progress in the Work, "what you took as yourself begins to look like a little prison-house far away in the valley beneath you." This is a vivid expression of the "third state of consciousness" or "self-remembering" as it is called. These flashes of greater consciousness are the unexpected results of the strenuous efforts made in order not to lose oneself in the rush of outer circumstances, to be cleansed from the acids of negativity, and to maintain a heightened awareness grounded in the present.

The student is to reach a point where he or she can make the choice not to react automatically to external stimuli. This requires going against the grain, against long established habits and self-indulgences. The question is as basic as: can you find the willpower to choose not to react angrily to something that makes you angry? Rather than being wasted in such an outburst, the energy accumulated through this effort can be available for a moment of intensified consciousness. Such a moment will flood you with peace or quiet joy or a sense of profound liberation.

Oddly enough, such rare and precious moments often come in very paradoxical events. When night is darkest, a shaft of light can suddenly breaks through. Self-remembering, combined with the insights of objective self-observation assists in the creation of a balanced individual who is not completely under the sway of his or her inborn nature and acquired habits. It is not possible to experience a vaster sense of reality if we are entirely under the dominance of the intellect to the exclusion of the emotional or the instinctive part of our nature and vice-versa. In attempting to make the "machine" work right, it is necessary to change attitudes and behavior developed over years of wrong functioning.

Ouspensky told his students that it is only when we realize that life is taking us nowhere that it begins to have meaning. This observation is not a philosophy, but a pragmatic realization which can fundamentally alter our perception of ourselves and of the world around us. Maurice Nicoll gives a hint of these first stages of real change in his Commentaries: "This gradual withdrawal of energy from the customary, easily resentful and brittle feeling of 'I' is accompanied by a gradual new and broader feeling of I, as if one were living in a larger place...It is like being introduced to a new civilization, to another form of life." He points out that by using the inner camera of self-observation, we begin to open a mind above the level of the sensual mind.

Here is where the psychological experiences of the Fourth Way begin to reveal their numinous and "religious" character. The same idea is found in the teachings of Karlfried Graf Durckheim which is informed by Zen Buddhism, Christian mysticism and psychotherapy. He writes of the experience of higher awareness in this way: "It is no longer the old I but a wider, more comprehensive one. We do not lose ourselves in it but, on the contrary, truly find ourselves. A new breathing space, scope and sphere of action opens up and we realize only then how confined we had been before, how imprisoned and isolated."

Durckheim also gives us a clear description of the first steps of inner development which are fundamental to all such instructions: "Practice on ourselves, in the physical and spiritual sense, is always of two kinds. It involves both the pulling-down of everything that stands in the way of our contact with Divine Being, and the building-up of a 'form' which, by remaining accessible to its inner life, preserves this contact and affirms it in every activity in the world."

Self-remembering, then, is a process of being lifted out of our ordinary sense of self into a purified, detached space well known to those long practiced in meditation. But in the Fourth Way this birth of new awareness can be accomplished while one crosses a city street or takes out the trash. Nevertheless, despite the practical approach of the Work, self-remembering remains as intangible and paradoxical as any spiritual exercise. Reminiscent of the Zen koan, Rodney Collin told his students that we cannot remember ourselves until we forget ourselves. And at the height of his powers of understanding, he united the Fourth Way with the wisdom of all times and places: "To feel beauty, to feel truth, that is self-remembering. Self-remembering is the awareness of the presence of God."

THE SPIRITUAL DIMENSION

The idea that we are not awake but live in a partial dream state from which we can awaken opens onto radically new horizons. The illusions we foster concerning ourselves melt under the light of increased consciousness and we awaken to new dimensions of reality which set us free. We are then able to relate to the world around us without the usual defenses, masks, and confusion which constitute much of human interaction. We become capable of a new kind of compassion.

Ultimately, this third state of consciousness, which is our birthright, frees us from the unnecessary agonies of a little

27

ego always struggling for self-importance and awakens us to immeasurable vistas of new insight and understanding. The world becomes a different place, we become far more than our imaginary selves ever dreamt of, and the potential for happiness, fulfillment, and genuine usefulness to humanity are now tangible realities. This use of attention is similar to the "watch of the heart" of early eastern Christian spirituality and the "remembrance of God" of the Sufi mystics.

To be aware of higher reality while dealing with ordinary reality requires an effort of awareness, detachment, concentration and insight which are the result of long practice. These experiences of vaster consciousness have been tasted by everyone in rare moments of our lives and our reminiscent of the wonder years of childhood. But despite the deep emotion or astonishing joy that accompanies them, they are always fleeting, ephemeral, and uncontrollable. The disciplines of the Work eventually make the practitioner receptive to longer, more frequent encounters with these regenerating and illuminating events.

These are the transformative moments that people have sought in drugs and voyages to exotic lands, in love and intense emotion. On the foundations of objective self-observation and liberation from constant entanglement (or identification) with circumstances of the outer world, these experiences become the oxygen of our souls. The mysterious and obscure passages of sacred scripture from all religions then begin to take on deeper meaning and each individual discovers for himself or herself those life-giving encounters with transcendent reality. Expressions such as "the kingdom of God" or "Nirvana" are then no longer lovely ideas but concrete, accessible experiences.

In proportion as we learn to remember ourselves, our actions acquire a meaning and consistency which is not possible as long as our attention moves only from one fascination to another. If we take seriously this state of awareness called self-remembering, many new possibilities open to us. But it does not take long to realize that there is an enormous resistance in ourselves against mastering this new state. We find that we have to give up all the more psychopathic ways of burning up our attention and energy which now seem such a necessary part of life--irritation, indignation, self-pity, all sorts of fears, and all the ways we hypnotize ourselves into satisfaction with things as they are.

The premise that we are not awake but live in a partial dream state opens entirely new horizons in dealing with our problems and the difficulties of other people. The release of the illusions we foster concerning ourselves frees us to relate to others without the usual defenses and masks which constitute much of human interaction.

At their core, the originators of the Fourth Way as we know it today were religious men in the true sense of the term. Work on oneself leads to a liberation which can be compared to the enlightenment and divinization of more religious methods. But writings on the Fourth Way have generally remained entirely secular with the notable exceptions of the works of Maurice Nicoll and Rodney Collin. Left with the exoteric dimension of the Work, the Fourth Way can be reduced to the development of personal powers and dehumanizing attitudes. To be somewhat liberated from mechanicalness and the illusion of unity can allow a person to manipulate those who are still caught in the tyranny of waking sleep.

The Fourth Way is meant ultimately to transcend even the Work's own magnificent thought structures so that every student can find for himself or herself the new life of a higher consciousness which constantly seeks to reach us if only we would make the effort to awaken and ready ourselves to receive its treasures of wisdom and regeneration.

Gurdjieff required that each person verify the teachings for themselves based on their personal observations and experiences. That is why he rarely mentioned the idea of "God" even though he called his teaching "esoteric Christianity." His task was to help people free themselves from all that is false and imaginary in order that they might become receptive to their higher self and enter uncharted dimensions of consciousness on their own through liberation from the tyranny of their ego.

Gurdjieff broke through the dogma of institutional religion and revealed the dynamic truth within the teachings. He made clear the psychological insights beneath the rust of rote repetition and blasphemous misuse of the words of enlightened teachers. His insistence on verification forced the student to come upon the stunning fact that life is indeed more than that which the senses perceive and to re-interpret spiritual insights in the context of their own lives. Belief was to give way to experience and experience to transformation so that the "new man" could emerge out of the ashes of rejected illusions.

It is for this reason that Gurdjieff was so merciless on his students. He crushed vanity and artifice, mocking those who thought they understood something. He differentiated between two forms of knowing: knowledge and understanding. The first is of the head, the second is that which takes root in our being and transforms us. He did indeed humiliate many egos stuffed with pride and broke people's confidence in their own importance.

A great library is now arising around this unique and extraordinary man. Some condemn him, some worship him, most praise his influence on seekers of the twentieth century. He remains an enigma, even a danger to those who would approach his transformative teachings without a compass. But there are some who have found their lives forever enlightened by exposure to this strange and complex man.

His colossal personal efforts, carried on in spite of a revolution and two world wars, and his desire to share the awakening he had found with seekers here in the West, will someday be recognized as one of the central events of our century.

Gurdjieff tore through our most cherished beliefs with astonishing force and irreverence, stung our vanities with brutal honesty, and called us to that ultimate journey toward the consciousness of who we are and who we are meant to be.

Behind the exotic masks of this oriental magician-rogue-teacher was great compassion. Children and animals sensed it, while seekers of all classes and types found healing and new life from his sometimes bizarre requirements. Gurdjieff came to wake us with uncompromising affection and assist us accessing our deeper selves. No one walks away unchanged from the teachings of this intense Master who has taught us to discover someone even more elusive than himself: the true nature of our being.

II
THE POWER OF SELF-OBSERVATION

The power of Self-Observation lies in the fact that it teaches us that we need not be fully captive of our behavior. Just becoming aware of muscle tension begins a process of relaxing them. Many of the great teachers state that this simple process of relaxing tense muscles is directly related to your spiritual state in the moment. Applying the simple act of awareness frees you to just BE in the moment. One can only begin that kind of inner liberation by a separation. If you are that tension, you cannot NOT be that. This is part of the magic of this idea of detachment which is found in all spiritual teachings and which is called in the Fourth Way "Inner Separation". The Work gives us those practical tools. It does not provide abstract platitudes but a how-to approach which begins with remembering some of these ideas in the midst of the daily rush in order to notice something about oneself. That noticing is the first step toward awakening.

The Work talks about our Many I's, the many parts of our being that we do not control. There are certain aspects of our being that have no interest in spirituality and evolution and will actually fight against it. One of them is our instinctive nature, which is interested in eating and staying warm. It handles our digestion and is a mind that has its own way of doing things. We cannot claim ownership of it or control it. Quite often it is in control of us and most often gets what it wants. As we apply this Work and try to make choices against forces within that have always had their way, we will experience resistance. We are a universe within. As above so below.

Maurice Nicoll says that we eventually learn -- as we become more aware of all of the elements of our inner being -- to walk carefully in the landscape of our being. There are certain places we should not let ourselves go into.

The crack in the wall of our state of sleep is precisely found in noticing. Something else becomes active and the more you develop that inner space the more you begin to enter a new dimension of presence. To notice that you are automatically repetitive means that something else is becoming active and beginning to see.

The more you develop that inner space that is not entirely ripped out of you by automatic reaction, the more you begin to enter a new dimension of presence, of awareness. Try to notice how thoughts that enter your mind are not your thoughts. Try to catch a moment when something in your mind has been "dumped in", such as a reaction to the radio or to what someone said. And yet we immediately assume that it is we who are thinking this because it is in our mind, and therefore it is us and we are one with it, when in fact it is a thought merely floating through the various frequencies that we are tuned into. If you saw a horror movie last night, and today you are suffering from a strange paranoia, try to notice the connection.

The early teachers of Christianity were extraordinarily aware of this phenomenon and developed a complex methodology for dealing with the inner life. They called it "the watch of the heart". They recognized that when thoughts entered and these feelings bubbled up, they had a choice to catch them at the point of recognition. If they were aware in the moment enough to say "here is a thought that I am not going to go with because if I let it enter me further and let it become an emotional feeling, it will eventually become an action manifested in the world." To cut that thought off at the source requires that it must be caught before it has such an impact on you.

This reality of the "state of waking sleep" as Gurdjieff called it, suggests that we are hardly any more conscious or in control as when we are asleep and that we in fact live mostly in a dream state. The aim is to become grounded in a deeper reality. We are so filled with this imaginary world, mainly through this imaginary sense of unity that we have about ourselves which blinds us to the inner panorama of our psychology, that we can only hope to chip away at it a little at a time. Though it is long-term Work, we are blessed by moments when we experience this freedom from our usual sense of self, our usual reactions to the world, and are able to have a moment of higher consciousness -- or awareness of the presence of God -- where peace, release, joy, gratitude for living can exist.

III
ON NON-IDENTIFICATION

The idea of non-identifying carries with it a depth of meaning that needs to be explored thoroughly in order to avoid misunderstanding. Its parallel can be found in other ideas related to spiritual evolution, such as detachment, freedom from desire, inner peace. The results of this effort are seen in the presence of sages and saints in all times and places.

Non-identification is ultimately self-transcendence. It requires us to overcome a fundamental self-interest that guides everyone's lives in order to accept passing circumstances, in order to remember the greater context in which our lives are taking place. We must become liberated from all that is connected with the selfishness with which we are born.

This condition is part of our natural make-up, as basic to us as the instinct to survive. The paradox is that spiritual and psychological survival requires the opposite. The maturing of the human character means turning one's attention to something greater than oneself. We all know people who have completely crystallized in the state of identification. It is a tragic dead-end that brings despair and solitude in its wake. Such persons equate the state of identification with their identity. Their negativity, their reactions from false personality are how they know themselves. They are not aware of other options. This Work reveals that in fact we do have other options of behavior.

To be identified means that we literally lose ourselves, lose our identity, in that with which we are identified. A new car gets a dent in it and we have an angry reaction -- we become the dent in the car, this is our reality. There is no sense of Self unaffected by this external event. To remember that Self -- which is the opposite of identification -- suggests that we are present to this moment of our lives and its link to the rest of our existence. We are the child that we once were, the youth, all of our life experience that we have acquired on this journey through time and space. This remembrance creates a density that is not dragged down or fragmented by the passing event with which we would otherwise be identified.

To be in a state of identification is a condition in which we find in everyone around us and in which we live and breathe and have our being. It is a total waste of life-force, it is imagination, self-indulgence, pettiness, unreality.

The serenity that is witnessed in the sages and saints of the past is not meant to be some rare or unique nobility of character. It is right alignment with reality. It is an achievable state for all of us. This Work takes us there step by step if we make persistent, right efforts. Non-identification has nothing to do with a disconnection of the emotional center, lack of compassion or interest in what is going on around us. In fact, to be non-identified gives one the widest scope of vision and makes possible a new awareness.

Non-identification pulls us out our black hole of distorted self-interest which gives us tunnel vision and keeps our psychology in the basement of its potential. It is very difficult work, as anyone will quickly discover upon making efforts to overcome identification. It demands moment by moment remembrance of Work ideas, of one's higher aims, and a constant return to inner separation from our automatic reactions and the tyranny of false personality and its infinite variety of self-gratifying desires. Finally, non-identification requires the capacity to accept necessary suffering, a fact that everyone must deal with in one way or another. To experience inner pain without falling victim to negativity (including self-pity) or becoming completely unbalanced by the surfacing of the emotional center as the only perspective on reality and is a sign of a new maturity of will and understanding.

At the apex of this level of being is the ability to find joy and gratitude for the gift of life even in the face of great turmoil, injustice, or tragedy. Living in that paradox creates a new quality of Self which transcends the ever-shifting scenery of temporal life. It is the groundwork of unity, constancy, and independence.

IV
SOME ANSWERS TO QUESTIONS

[STUDENT: Gurdjieff said in "*In Search of the Miraculous*" that connection with the large accumulator can only come through the emotional center. The other three centers feed only on the small accumulators. Therefore, "*the aim must be on the development of the emotional center*".(p.235) Naturally, no further instructions are given. My question: Other than to refuse indulgence of negative emotion, what may one do in a positive manner to connect with the large accumulator? Is it effort? And if so, of what kind? I find the text somewhat nebulous on this point (as I do others).

[TN] The above quote from G. is a critical clue for those who seek to evolve. He is telling us that a key breakthrough toward transformation comes through the emotional center.
In our stimulus-response behavior, the emotional center is primarily made of negative energy, like and dislike, crowd emotion (jack of hearts) and so forth. Yet its potential is to be an instrument of cognition. Through intelligent emotion comes intuitive knowing, conscience, remorse, awareness of our responsibility to the Universe, and other qualities of awareness that cannot be easily put into words. The reference to the large accumulator is merely a technical term for tapping into more high voltage, refined energy than that with which we normally operate. But we do not work on the emotional center in order to tap into the larger accumulator. It is the result of the right use of the emotions. In those moments, we can detect another quality of energy circulating within us. This is not the aim, but the by-product.

41

For instance, you can verify that an act of self-transcendent kindness toward another person or an effort of real forgiveness will generate another kind of energy within you. That is the least of the issues involved here. The Work is not about energy but about becoming. The other question is the more important one -- the positive uses of emotion. Work on negative emotions must occur because we are so soil and rendered opaque by this constant misuse of emotional energy. If we seek any significant change, we must perform these efforts of undoing wrong work, which is almost a permanent condition for many people.

Work on positive emotion is also important because it introduces us to the potential of higher states. For example, making the effort to not identify will produce a subtle emotional quality which can be defined as positive. Or seeing beauty -- such as the Autumn leaves -- without interference by the ups and downs of our circumstances, but being present to that grander reality brings forth positive emotion. External considering, giving no thought to oneself but caring for the needs of another, is another key way of working on positive emotion.

Making the effort to not expose oneself to the toxic stimuli that are all around us (media and so forth which often generates negative emotion) leaves energy available for work on positive emotion. Learning to accept what IS and finding a certain contentment in being present in the moment generates positive emotion. Being freed from self-absorption enough to sense the state of others and perceive what is needed for right action in specific circumstances is another form of positive emotion. Intentionally feeding one's higher emotions (quiet reading versus watching a football game) helps to develop positive emotions. After awhile one will want to live there as much as possible and leave behind the chaos, self-indulgence and unpleasantness of the misuse of the emotional center.

The sense of one's connection with a vaster life and gratitude for being alive and a witness to the phenomenon of conscious existence in the Universe generates positive emotion. Perhaps you can see that all of these approaches tie in to the state of self-remembering for which positive emotion is fundamental. You will also note that divided attention, knowing what is going on within oneself, getting to know one's nature, must be done in a way that paradoxically frees us from self-absorption. This liberation from pettiness and sleep opens onto a greater reality that is the primary path toward positive emotion. This path can lead to profound spiritual experience which each must find for themselves.

***

[STUDENT: Court proceedings resulted in the most unjust, draconian solution imaginable for a client. During the proceeding, I sought to observe myself, remember myself. Things have changed inside. It does not seem like the end of the world. The clients are apoplectic. Life is school.]

[TN] You can also observe (in the case to which you refer that "your being attracts your life"), that the energy of life driving everything is negativity, the "law of accident," mechanics producing predictable responses, everyone's total identification with every event, and therefore complete lack of relativity (sleep). Injustice exists because of sleep.

There is another level of being that includes an increased perspective and understanding born of effort and experience in the Work. It includes relativity, compassion, and acceptance. Its nature is not that of self-interest and consequently it is liberated and can be objective, clear and unidentified seeing. Such seeing is not emotionally dead or repressed, but serene and wise.

This is what is created through doing this inner Work. The psychological practices and ideas gradually clear away all the wrong work of mechanical psychology (the lies and dirt of negativity in all its forms, self-interest, vanity, inner considering, pictures of oneself, lying, pride and everything else the Work tells us to observe). This process strips the personality (ego)and leaves one feeling vulnerable and rather without a "real personality" to replace the dying false personality. One does become withdrawn.

This is a critical stage in the Work. What this emptiness should create in you is humility. Not self-condemnation, but self-transcendence and real self-remembering. Humility expands understanding which begets meaning.

A new Self is born with observing "I". It is the Real Self and will grow stronger and become more present with the continued practice of self-observation. With practical work and verifying experience, one's awareness expands. Continuing sincere efforts can expand one's consciousness permanently, but what you sacrifice to reach this point is all that you believe yourself to be and all interest in seeking personal gratification. Not everyone is willing to pay such a high price.

Those who are courageous enough to continue will find valuation of the Work to be the only third force needed. Therefore, the new faculty in one's psychology (that of developing consciousness) is fed by the power of right valuation. The path of evolution is upward toward illumination, through the sight of understanding, toward finer and finer energies that cannot support the weight of violence. This path leads away from the automatic animal level of being toward enlightened intentionality.

***

[STUDENT: What does the taste of REALIZATION feel like?]

[TN] Assuming that by the "taste of realization" you are referring to the presence of awakened consciousness (also known as self-remembering), the taste is familiar.

This state feels as though one is seeing everything from a higher perspective which includes a broader vista. Connections are seen that cannot be recognized from a lower level. It feels like unified, undifferentiated, utterly unique, serene selfhood. One does experience something of that "peace which passes all understanding." The reason it is beyond understanding is that such a state of serenity occurs despite paradoxical circumstances. It "makes no sense" in the reality of the second state of consciousness. This state includes acceptance, serenity, humility, resolution of paradoxes, sometimes deep joy and gratitude. It comes to us as both a gift and as a result of our efforts.

One feels as valuable as any other creation in the Universe and as transient. One feels intuitively connected with all of life. One's sense of identity shifts and a truer, purer quality of self replaces the narrow, identified, second state. A sense of harmony arises from this new perspective and understanding. This experience can form a permanent faculty in one's psychology where that consciousness is present. The Work calls it "an organ of perception" formed by understanding, growth in being, illumination. That level of consciousness is available not only ahead of us in time but above us in time now.

The self-evolution of the figures in Fourth Way literature undoubtedly possessed that faculty which nevertheless does not eliminate the reality of continued effort. This is why their comments are most often focused on the difficulties of achieving change. But at some point, for those who persist, there are breakthroughs and one begins to "be able to do", which also means being "able to be". Results are not only possible but verifiably achievable. However, the great mass of humanity (and of seekers) does not wish to awaken.

***

[TN] An important development along this path is to notice that we live in different states of consciousness. This is not as obvious as it sounds. I am not referring here to moments of happiness in contrast to times of depression but to a state of being that puts us in touch with a deeper reality. Perhaps you have had moments of experiencing such a liberation that comes from these higher states of being. Moments of great joy, or gratitude for being alive, or while standing before a scene of great beauty. Moments when our awareness is lifted beyond the knots and tensions of our worries and concerns and we are free to enjoy the experience of being here now and happy to be alive. These are higher states of being.

You may have had such experiences as children when we were less weighed down by the things that now preoccupy us. And maybe you think that those times of bliss and wonder are gone forever along with the other delights of childhood. But that is not the case. We are meant to dwell permanently in this habitat of the soul where higher consciousness dwells. It is possible to taste and live this joy and freedom, this inner awakening, even during rush hour, even at the office, even when circumstances around you are difficult. Let's take a look at our everyday state of consciousness. Teachings on this subject describe our usual condition of consciousness as a state of sleep.

Though we all believe that we are fully conscious in every moment of our lives, the fact is that most of our existence is spent "on automatic." We are stimulus-response organisms: something happens to us and we react.

We think we choose how we behave, but most often we are simply one giant knee-jerk reaction to whatever comes our way: --your child disobeys you and you get angry -- you spill a drink on yourself and you're embarrassed -- the red light lasts too long and you're impatient the list is endless, from morning till night. It's the world of stress, of ups and downs, of good days and bad days, of insecurity, inconsistency, unreliability. It's the world we know so well. If you think the word "sleep" is a strange way to describe our condition, just think back on the last time you observed someone watching television.

The vacant stare, the loose jaw...we are virtually hypnotized by life around us, drawn out of ourselves and no more able to make choices than when we are in the middle of a dream. Things happen and we respond according to our programming. It's all consuming. Our first obstacle is therefore our wrong perspective on our lives. We take ourselves for granted.

We think we know who we are. We believe that we are one and the same person all the time. But take a closer look and dare to be honest with yourself. When you're really hungry, the you that is hungry is in charge in charge. When you're irritable, the you that's irritated is the boss. When you're tired, when you're excited, when you're mad, each mood and desire is in control. Where is the unity of oneself in all that? Again, we function in a stimulus-response manner that takes away our capacity to be unified as individuals. We can't count on ourselves to be the same person from one moment to the next. The person who decides the night before to get up early in the morning is not the one who has to turn off the alarm and roll out of bed. That person has a very different idea of what he or she wants to do. To make matters worse, each of these impulses that claims to be the whole person is separated by blinders. They do not know each other. When we are our happy-go-lucky selves, we don't remember the mean-tempered one. Our condition of multiplicity is further complicated by the fact that we live so much of our life in imagination. Consider how much time is spent worrying about the future, or fretting over the past.

Think of all the day dreaming that goes on in your head. And look at how we bounce from one thought to the next without any intentionality or purpose: someone mentions a word (like blue) and our mink takes us off on a tangent that gets more and more tangled until we no longer have any idea how we got to a certain mood or idea. So in our ordinary state of consciousness we are made of many disconnected selves, we are pulled to and fro by imagination and unintentional thoughts and yet we think we are in full control of ourselves. Now we come to an even more fundamental problem: our essential nature, that which we truly are -- the sensitivities, the gifts, the inclinations we were born with -- is generally repressed at an early stage of our life. As we encounter the world around us, the essence of who we are becomes covered over by the development of our personality.

Here again, we take for granted that our personality is who we genuinely are. But our personality is rarely related to our essence and our natural inclinations. Throughout our pre-teen, adolescent, and early adulthood years we have, both consciously and unconsciously, built up defense mechanisms to survive the pain of dealing with life. We have developed masks to protect ourselves or to manipulate others. Furthermore, we have absorbed into our idea of ourselves the images that our culture tells us are the acceptable way of being a man or a woman. We have accumulated the imitations or our parents, our peers and our environment.

In a word, we have covered over our essential nature to such an extent that we have to virtually undertake an archeological exploration in order to rediscover ourselves. In order to find the habitat of our soul, in order to live right, we have to be aligned with our real self. But there are powerful forces in the way. The greatest among them is negativity in all its forms: irritation, anger, impatience, depression, hatred, vengeance, jealousy, envy, and resentment. These are all poisons within us that cause us so much unnecessary suffering and use up so much of our energy, our life-force. We can't have to live like that! Even though it seems that everyone around us indulges in these negative forms of behavior, they are not the only way to live. Imagine how different your life would be without the constant stress of these wretched feelings. But that entails dealing with our greatest foe: our vanity. Vanity is not merely primping in the mirror.

It causes us to spend much of our life in self-interested activity, in thinking about ourselves, in having to be right, in asserting ourselves over others, in stubbing our pride over this or that. Vanity causes us to have a false idea of ourselves a false sense of self-importance, along with a perverse distortion of our attention. Everything becomes me, me, me. So much grief and misery comes from this petty self-centeredness that disfigures our humanity. We are our own greatest source of suffering as long as we live in this state of sleep that is ruled by automatic behavior, a self-centered focus, negative emotions, multiple selves trying for control, and misperceptions of who we truly are. So what is the true Self found in higher states? It is the life-force beyond our mistaken notion of ourselves that is seeking to come through us and accomplish its work of goodness in the world. It is that mysterious "presence" that can overcome solitude, meaninglessness, and despair. Moreover, not only is it always there -- deep within -- but it is seeking us more than we are seeking it.

***

[STUDENT: I have tried to keep watch, and take note of, the shifting "I's" and that shape-shifting 'person' behind them. This, I think, is valuable from an observing point of view, but then may be no more than a sleepy little cataloging activity and ends up giving the phantom selves a credence they do not deserve.]

[TN] Observing multiplicity is valuable information. Whether any Work practice becomes formatory or authentic depends entirely on the sincerity and effort of the student. It can become formatory cataloging, but it needn't. It can over time recognize recurring I's and groups of I's. In seeing their repetitiveness, one can feel less identified, knowing that it is mechanical behavior, knowing that a particular group of I's always leads to a particular psychological state that needs to be avoided for the sake of this Work. There is a wealth of knowledge to be gained by observing one's own multiplicity, including a sense of what is behind all of that shifting sand of personalities. Seeing the continuous activity of changing I's, you begin have a sense of WHAT is seeing this activity and consequently develop a stronger sense of separation from the multiplicity. At some point you will be able to decide which I's to give your attention to and which I's to disempower. In truth, we must see that level of changing I's as a veneer that must be removed so that something more permanent and stable can be present.

***

[STUDENT: To verify, see, feel, that there are many I's, I must be able to hold together to very different I's .It does not need to be so complicated or strained. Opposite I's and contradictory I's are self-evident. There is a [ME] who wants to study a subject intensely and a [ME] who wants to lay on the couch and watch television. One who sets the aim of getting up early in the morning, and one who wakes up to the alarm and hates the idea of getting up. It will help for you to perceive the appearance of different centers --intellectual, emotional, instinctive, moving -- as they vie for temporary control and satisfaction of their desires. The non-involvement and careful watch of Observing I will lift you out of the chaos of multiplicity and eventually anchor your sense of self outside of the hypnotizing power and attraction of the many I's stimulated in us in countless ways. To me, this is a very big thing. When it happens, if at all, it burns akin to a feeling of deep shame and I feel a disorientation.]

[TN] Remorse of conscience is an important ingredient in our development. But as Rodney Collin astutely points out -- once we have tasted it, we must move on. There is no value in wallowing in remorse. It is bitter, no doubt, but can be a major third force for growing in this Work.

[STUDENT: But then when I actually try to apply the words, apparently nothing occurs and I am discouraged. It is necessary to burn up the intruders who have taken up residence in this 'house'. To hold them firmly in the light of consciousness so that, through the light and contradictions, they are burned and destroyed.]

[TN] The ancient ones of early eastern Christianity taught that, in relation to intruding thoughts, we should be so vigilant that as soon as they "show their heads, like a serpent appearing through a hole, we must cut it off"!This is a potent use of the "stop exercise" which is also meant to halt the entry and influence of I's that seek to claim our identity. The more you live in a more quiet inner place (an inner sanctuary) where features cannot take over, the more you will see the difference between passing thoughts and feelings and your deeper self.

It is subtle business, but most certainly can be achieved. Among other things, don't take yourself so seriously. Relax and try to live at a different pace. Find some silence between the notes.

V

RESPONSES TO A SEEKER

Deep within our buried conscience is some awareness of what is right in the presence of God and as part of our true destiny. We cannot do this extraordinary Work—which is the heart of all esoteric and spiritual teaching given to humanity—without a sense that there is something higher than oneself. This is where our magnetic center, the small part of us that has led us on some kind of spiritual search for meaning and purpose, is especially valuable. There are 'I's within us that know there is more to life than self-gratification, self-love, self-interest. These 'I's yearn for a mysterious inner liberation where a new quality of consciousness and of daily living can take place. This is no fantasy. It is the very reason why we were created as self-evolving beings. We have a job to do and it is called "metanoia" or transformation of mind.

There is no doubt that we cannot do this on our own. Perhaps you've heard the sayings "when the student is ready, the teacher appears", or "seek and you will find". All persons who enter a real search for something greater discover that help becomes available. In this Teaching, we are told that there is help available to us but we cannot receive it in our current condition or state. We must enter the Third State of Consciousness in order to "catch the rope" that is handed down to us. This Third State is Self-Remembering and it is characterized by non-identification, inner separation, external considering. It is the state of detachment found in Zen or in Christian mysticism. One has managed to step out of personality and its many petty requirements and found a place where a certain transcendent peace exists. This is a place that is familiar to us. We were all born with some knowledge of this in our essence, but life and its hardships blinded us as we developed personality and its defense mechanisms.

One of the fundamental aims of the Work is the purification of the emotional center. Our emotions are meant to be instruments of cognition, not endless generators of self-emotions that toss us from one state to another. One can intuit the state of another and the sense of what right action is needed in a moment through the proper use of the emotional center. But to do this one must break with the wrong work that has been unconsciously instilled in us. This is not impossible and in fact is a requirement of being a real adult. We must break from the "sins of the fathers". Regardless of what was done to you, your responsibility is to not pass it on to another generation. You must gather the strength of character and presence of mind to say before all that is holy—"This wrong behavior stops here."

The Work and all the great religions require self-sacrifice, the crucifixion of the self-interested person (the "old man"). You have an opportunity to become a new person, to be good to your wife in spite of everything, to forgive her, to forgive yourself for the sake of your children. You have access to special tools that can help you have compassion for her and assist you in understanding yourself (the two go together).

If you make the effort to not go with 'I's that you know are from old ways that do not serve your aim of evolving and awakening, you will reap the reward both for yourself and for your family. You will experience an increase of marvelous energy, an empowering of your will to go with the higher in yourself, and a new peace of mind. There is no future in staying on the road of old habits and wrong behavior. There is only unspeakable misery. You have been given the chance to save yourself and your family from such dark despair. Your past does not need to haunt you or control you. You have a chance to acquire wisdom, to incarnate goodness, to find fulfillment by doing right.

But it is spiritual warfare and you have to make definite choices. So it is with everything in life, from the ordinary business of dieting to accomplishing things in education and business. It is all the more necessary in the spiritual realm.

Seek out Third Force to strengthen your aims. Find kindred spirits where you live—other students, a wise counselor in a church. Somewhere there awaits another person who will help you if you truly wish to stay on the path of spiritual transformation.
Do not be discouraged. Do not allow yourself to fall into unnecessary negative emotions. We have all suffered and made mistakes. Above all, never give up. It is time for a new thing to happen. Enter the path of becoming and there will be light in your future.

REGARDING AIMS

For a long time, simply the aim of seeing what is occurring is a major one indeed. Eventually, you move from recognizing negativity (for instance) and its toxic impact on your life to making the effort of not expressing it, and then to making the choice in the moment to transform it into neutral energy which is used for generating a more serene state of consciousness. This is a prototype for the stages, whether dealing with inner considering, negative imagination, false personality, features, etc.

Clearly, the early stages require the painful labor of seeing oneself honestly in the light of objective observation. That seeing alone will reveal extraordinary new data, such as how much of one's psychology is imitated from parents and cultural influences. Also, to witness the amount of negativity in one's reactions creates a desire for developing the will to change.
I would recommend the more personal approach of discovering your own specific "wrong work" based on the teaching and dealing with particular details one at a time. One classic element would be the indulgence in daydreaming which often creates worries about the future based on imagination. This is a giant leakage of energy and can be seen for what it is very quickly.

Simply witnessing your inner reactions with people and circumstances will give you mountains of information about yourself.

Gathering that material will lead to being able to make different choices in the moment of reaction.

So the simple aim of seeing without identification is one that needs to be primary for a good while. Second, focus on the issue of negativity. Try to not express it and see what happens.

ANSWERS TO QUESTIONS

QUESTION:
What I do see is that my mind is not sufficient to solve its own problems, and if that is a correct observation, I wonder what I can do about it all?

RESPONSE:
Knowing this is already an important step. This is where Nicoll would say that one needs the "Neutralizing Force of the Work" without which we cannot change. Our life is generally lived under the impact of the neutralizing force of life—outer circumstances, inward attitudes and illusions continually shape our behavior.

Making the Work and its ideas the neutralizing force means that we seek to no longer be determined by the same things. Our personality is made passive so that the Work ideas can influence our actions and understanding.

QUESTION:
Somehow I feel very blocked in my mind, and I don't know what to do or what to say, or what to ask next.

RESPONSE:
I would suggest a slow but regular reading of the Commentaries. Take an idea and seek to apply it to yourself. Learn from the observations and obstacles. Verify its truth for yourself. Let it help you discover something about yourself. Let it help you seek the inner space of Self-Remembering which lifts you beyond the questions and answers and becomes an answer itself—a state of peace, even bliss, where one is no longer devoured by the 'I's (thoughts and emotions) that flood us constantly.

QUESTION:
In spite of the many thousand things it can think and know, I feel there is something important that it cannot know, and does not know.

RESPONSE:
This is important and opens you to the possible experience of something higher than yourself. The Work tells us that our higher centers are continually active and available to help us but we live only in the lower centers and cannot hear them. To not identify, to practice inner separation with whatever is going on inside and outside of you, opens the door to receiving help.
Help is available. It is we who are not.
You are on the right track by knowing that you do not know.

QUESTION:
How can I learn to know which are the good 'I's, as I practice self-observation? ...but I would like to know a little more about how I can identify and support the good 'I's.

RESPONSE:
This is the very important work of discernment (the famous "diakrisis" of early eastern Christian teaching) where one learns to discern by inner taste the good from the bad within.
In relation to the Work, you should have some assistance in telling the difference between I's that wish to work and those that clearly don't.
This can be a simple matter of honestly observing what is trying to take center stage.

QUESTION:
For instance, is external consideration a way to do this?

RESPONSE:
This effort would certainly call forth the I's that wish to evolve in this Work. A certain self-sacrifice is required and this is always against the current of False Personality.
This is a good insight.

Seek to establish inner silence at times (for a definition, see the terminology on the website). This will help to control the parts of you that do not wish to work.

QUESTION:
Should contradictions be viewed as blocking or promoting self-remembering?

RESPONSE:
The awareness of contradictions within oneself is critical to the beginning of real self-knowledge. This is where one verifies that one is not unified but a multiplicity and therefore has no real will. This perception is itself a moment of higher consciousness that can create authentic self-observation and enough liberation from the many I's to generate self-remembering.
Learning about buffers means entering the painful waters of seeing oneself with harsh honesty. This is the beginning of the weakening of False Personality.

QUESTION:
Does not contradiction also works to promote, rather than block, these two processes?

RESPONSE:
Contradictions do not promote, but interfere with the development of the Work. They are one of the greatest blocks to self-change. Awareness of contradictions is necessary to even know why there is a need for this Work. But that is the only way they "contribute" to the process of the Work. Contradiction is the opposite of the aim of the Work, which is internal unification around conscious understanding. That allows the reception of new influences and the capacity to do right action in the world.

QUESTION:
Now, this is the question I feel that I must ask you now: is it correct to practice self-remembering in the way that Ouspensky suggests here, or is there something that I have missed, concerning the way I shall practice it?

RESPONSE:

Your intuition that something has been missed is correct. This stems, in part, from Ouspensky himself. I am assuming here that you do not look upon Ouspensky as an infallible super human (as many followers inevitably do, especially in the case of Gurdjieff who was a much more impressive person). The quote you shared from Ouspensky strikes me now, some twenty-three years after taking it as objective truth, in the following manner:

Ouspensky was supremely intellectual, a man of mind first and foremost. He was that rare type who was centered in the intellectual part of the intellectual center. This explains his extremely dry and meticulously analyzed approach to something utterly spiritual. In my view, the statement you quoted on self-remembering fails miserably to grasp the essence of the concept, because it is approached in such a rational, scientific manner. Self-remembering is not divided attention, just like a house is not its cement foundation. Ouspensky has reduced it here in this comment to the point of being unrecognizable.

Other important students like Nicoll and Rodney Collin were better able to express the meaning of this term. Collin especially made it clear on an intuitive level. To paraphrase him, he said that self-remembering means to forget oneself, and moreover, that self-remembering means to remember God.

To qualify my criticism of Ouspensky, I would simply point to the end of his life where he told his students to "abandon the system", where he began to speak of the "Jesus Prayer" as a means of self-remembering, and where he was known to spend long nights drinking vodka alone.

Remember the idea of bringing the mind into the heart? I would suggest that this brilliant man may not have (at least publicly) managed to do that.

I would suggest that self-remembering is closer to Buddhist mindfulness than to divided attention. It is similar to the later only because one is free from what is going on around or going on inside one. Self-remembering is a leap upwards out of identification and into a realm that brings "peace that passes understanding", new insight, compassion, and ultimately unconditional love.

I spent many years struggling with this idea as well. Perhaps it is best not to complicate it too much or one will forever be twisting and bending one's mind over it. Self-remembering is the English translation of what Gurdjieff named in French "le rappelle de soi". That verb ('rappeller') has more to do with bringing back into awareness a quality of being which was ours before we became lost in the madness that is called adult life.

Remember also the perennial wisdom of making "effortless efforts". It requires a certain relaxation and peace to bring forth a different state of consciousness.

QUESTION:
I have a feeling that there is something that blocks me from bringing the mind into the heart, although I can't exactly put the finger at it.

RESPONSE:
This is a specific technical phrase from the Early Fathers. It could be translated in Work language to "intelligent emotion" or emotional cognizance coming from a higher use of the Emotional Center (particular the intellectual part of the Emotional Center, also known as the King of Hearts in the coded symbol of the cards).

QUESTION:
Could it be that False Personality feels frightened to bring the mind to the heart, and instead does everything in its power to bring the heart into the mud?

RESPONSE:
This may be a case of the nature of your machine being a man number three, centered in the intellect. Such persons do have trouble balancing their proper functioning so that emotion is more active as an instrument of perception (and compassion). Intellectually-centered persons respond to other people's pain with rational analysis rather than empathy.
Self-Remembering requires the activation of the Emotional Center

(see Nicoll's writings in Volume 2 on this matter).

QUESTION:
There is a central dilemma here that I don't know exactly how to solve: Shall I separate from the feeling of fright in this case? An alternative would be to go into the feeling, facing it, and go through it, but being aware that it is False Personality that makes it all up.

RESPONSE:
Fear is a topic and form of wrong work on which much is written. Most of all, you might want to engage your Intellectual Center when that feeling arises and think of it as negative imagination. This can free you from its power.
Also, think of that phrase "mind into heart" more simply as a type of conscious awareness that integrates intelligence and emotion in a manner that unifies, uplifts, and intensifies perception. You may also want to put this idea on the "back burner" for awhile so that it is not confusing to the more fundamental ideas expressed in the Work.

QUESTION:
First of all, could it be that the heart should be taken almost literal, to refer to the rhythms of the heart beat, i.e. a deep connection with bodily states, in case it would be something very concrete to "listen to the heart"?

RESPONSE:
The answer is no, the heart has understood in the teachings of the Early Fathers is the inner eye of the soul, the center of our being. The solar plexus is the location of the emotional center, so one could say that the heart can be equated with the source of emotions. A further definition, although more complex, is that the "heart" is known in ancient philosophy as the "nous". Here is a definition of that word by Robin Amis in his book "A Different Christianity":
"What then is the nous? This is experienced as that single organ of consciousness which contains all our knowledge in itself, not verbal or diagrammatic knowledge, but direct knowledge, entirely different from the descriptions and definitions that with most people pass for knowledge. This distinction is essentially of the unwritten tradition, as

it is one of those things that really cannot be adequately conveyed in writing without the aid of inspiration or spiritual intuition."

This barely touches on the importance of this term as it relates to "metanoia" and I would recommend that sometime you obtain a copy of Robin Amis' book. He is a longtime teacher of the Fourth Way, now informed by the work of Mouravieff, and is also a dear friend.

More specifically, it is critical to not interfere with the functioning of your physical body (such as breathing, etc) without more knowledge. The best thing to do in that area is focus of attention, relaxation, separation. Also, in regards to emotions, know that the true purpose of the emotional center is to be an "instrument of cognition". In other words, if we can overcome the wrong work of our emotions, they become a sensitive form of intuitive sight and wisdom. This is one reason it is so important to cleanse them of negative emotion, imagination, and all the chaos that they bring.

Inner purification is indeed a goal of the Work. "The pure in heart will see God" remains a cosmic and practical Truth. This inner cleansing does require special work on the emotions, but the Fourth Way starts us with the intellect which is easier to control than the speed of emotional response. To remember certain ideas and apply them leads to understanding the wrong use of emotion and eventually to making choices and using will power when they arise. Saying "This is not I" when a silly feeling arises can help to find a separate space that is not flooded by the wild swings of our emotions. Helping to quiet the heart might be a better way to look at the matter. The Fathers have a mysterious saying: "Bring the mind into the heart", which on one level means bringing intelligence to the emotions and emotional quality to the intelligence.

For now, you might continue the exercise of not expressing negative emotion so that you can at least develop some will over them and observe how useless and damaging they are. That will lead to the first steps of purification and freedom.

QUESTION:
How can I maintain an adequate inner attitude (Work attitude) in the

midst of so many external demands?

RESPONSE:
It is correct to understand that the Fourth Way is a spiritual path that is specifically aimed at taking place in the midst of life, as opposed to other ways, such as the way of the monk. This is why Gurdjieff called it the way of the "sly man" (le ruse in French, which translates better as the "smart" one) because someone in the Work learns to benefit from all that life throws at him, whether good or bad.
This is also why it is called the way of "Understanding" because it requires the wisdom to deal with external events and one's own psychology in order to produce something fruitful for one's spiritual awakening.

Self-Observation is the key. Even if you react wrongly (according to the Work) to a situation, the ability and knowledge to recognize this actually feeds your development in the Work. All information is useful. It is not about "behaving in the right way". You can learn a great deal in a moment of negativity about the misuses and wastes of energy, the value of not identifying, the opportunity to make other choices, the reason to put things in a larger perspectives, the limitations of your old habits and imitations, etc.
So whether False Personality rules the day or not, you can still be harvesting a great deal each and every moment that you make the effort to apply Work ideas. This is also true in observing others and seeing their sad state of affairs due to functioning in a state of Sleep.

Don't expect results from yourself. It is important to recognize the reality of your situation. We are prisoners of our dysfunctional psychology and we must realize over and over again how damaging is the state of Sleep and the tyranny of Personality.
Eventually we begin to develop "True Personality" which allows us to function appropriately in life, but with intention, purpose, and will.
Each moment is the best of opportunities to learn about your condition, the human condition from the viewpoint of the Work, and to verify the authenticity and potential of the Work ideas.

QUESTION:
Is it a good idea to write down observations on a more or less regular basis? Could that be a way to make the "recording" more effective? Or are there other elements in the process of self-observation that could be missing, which should be included?(What about self-remembering?)

RESPONSE:
I recommend that you look up material from Maurice Nicoll on "Work Memory". This is essentially a new faculty that retains insights from Observing I and begins to build a new perspective on one's mechanical nature. This requires time, of course, and continued efforts as recurrent observations begin to form an "image" of one's particular wrong work, and ultimately of one's Chief Feature—the axis around which Personality operates.
Writing things down may be helpful, certainly. But more important is the objective honesty that takes place in the moment of perception. It will not take long to recognize the familiar taste of certain recurring states.

As for Self-Remembering, this is a different activity than Self-Observation. It is important to attempt it several times a day, when you intentionally leave behind all thought and separate yourself from the ordinary involvement with life. This is the "first conscious shock" that the Work speaks of. In the long run, it enables us to deal entirely differently with incoming impressions. But first we must know how it is that we deal with them to begin with.

QUESTION:
...as if personality have wanted to drag me down in the mud.

RESPONSE:
You will note as time goes by that False Personality will in fact defend itself. So will the Instinctive Center. After a few victories, you will find harder resistance manifesting. Sometimes, it will be as simple (and obvious) as falling asleep every time you try to read material on the Work.
This is why the great Teachers of eastern Christianity (for instance,

Theophan the Recluse from 19th century Russia) always emphasize that one must continue on with zealous perseverance. You might find his work "Inner Warfare" especially helpful.

QUESTION:
Somehow it is always easier to destroy than build up something.

RESPONSE:
Insightful wisdom.

QUESTION:
How could I grow stronger in inner separation?

RESPONSE:
Find a "third force", that is, ways to reinforce your desire to sustain effort in this Work. Don't let much time go by without feeding that part of yourself that wants to make these efforts. If one does not increase, one will decrease. Christ says: "He who puts his hand to the plow and looks back is not worthy of the Kingdom."
Know that you must compromise with your Instinctive Center. Give it a "cookie" when you have required effort from it (advice from Gurdjieff himself). Make an aim and keep it small and achievable. Return to it each day without remorse for forgetting. Don't let negativity creep into your Work I's. Self-observation does not work if it makes you negative.

Remember that ultimately this is spiritual work and that there is help. As Winston Churchill said: "Never, never give up." (Because the unexamined life is not worth living.)
You will have breakthroughs or this Work would not have found you.

QUESTION:
There are two questions that I would like to make:
1. Is it correct to describe all these different aspects of my behavior as 'I's, in the sense of the Work?

RESPONSE:
Yes, all of these thoughts come from the makeup of personality, which is known as "false" or "acquired". This means that our ways of responding to things are learned unconsciously and are therefore subjective perspectives on Reality. The more they are separated from, the more their source can be seen. The key here is learning the art of inner separation.

QUESTION:
2. What shall I do with all these sub-personalities once I have begun to observe them?

RESPONSE:
Leave them be. Just don't "touch them" as Nicoll says. Don't let them take center stage and claim themselves as your Real Self or fundamental identity.

QUESTION:
But still I have this nagging feeling that I am not doing enough in the Work, or that I am not doing it in the "right" way, and I think that is the feeling that troubles me right now.

RESPONSE:
Self-observation takes a long time. It both creates new information about yourself and a new inner space which becomes independent of outer circumstances and of inner psychological conditioning. These I's cannot be removed, certainly not instantly. Some are useful for general activity. One must learn to make "effortless efforts" as Zen Buddhism speaks about. The Work is about using "attention" with more consciousness.

QUESTION:
And because I must study a lot in order to finish these studies, it is a great "enemy" to the Work, and I don't know how to do with it.

RESPONSE:
Keep it simple. When it is time to read, read. Focus the use of self-observation on times that bring wrong work, not on times when you

are doing what needs to be done.

Moments of self-remembering at the right time will make the fruits of the Work evident. You can also verify the truth of these ideas in observing both yourself and others. Also remember what Gurdjieff said: "Patience is the mother of will. If you have no mother, how can you be born?"

QUESTION:

Is the transformation of impressions also a way to transform energy (as your letter perhaps suggests), i.e. to gradually take energy from personality in order to build up new being, as you expressed it? That would mean that if I keep silent, if I stay passive, if I realize that I cannot do and in this way transform impressions , then personality would gradually be loosing strength, because it would be operating with less energy?

RESPONSE:

The transformation of impressions is a particular dimension of the Work, one especially studied in the "school" known as "The Fellowship of Friends". I wonder if you are familiar with them. Be sure to stay away if you find a link with them—they are without question a dangerous cult, led by a criminal sociopath. However, some of the Work ideas came through, and one was this idea of transforming impressions. Impressions is here understood as what is perceived in the outside world, i.e. visual perception. As one becomes more sensitive to energies and more discerning of higher or denser "vibrations" through liberation from wrong work within, it becomes possible to "feed" oneself finer food through intentionally receiving finer impressions. For instance, a particular inner state is created when watching a horror movie. It is evident even to sleeping machines that there is something toxic taken in to us. In the Work, this is most significant because it is very literally poisoning ourselves and damaging our efforts to evolve. Negativity is contagious.

On the other hand, if you visit a museum, your inner state will be impacted by finer energies that will in fact lighten your state and place you in a higher emotional state that bring you closer to a different state of consciousness. This is advanced Work as it requires a good deal of sensitivity to one's inner psychological country, and the differences there so well described by Nicoll. If you work in a barren or grim environment, one pleasant image can influence the quality of your inner state. This is the use of impressions.

As for the transformation of impressions, you are correct in deducing that passivity to personality is a first step. Neutralizing the negative energy of someone's nasty comments to you, or keeping your own negative reaction to this event from taking over your emotions, is indeed the beginning of transformation. In the long run, this transformation becomes potent when you can actually make the choice to not be negative in a difficult moment, to not be victimized by vanity and habit. Then the energy created by the event generates a moment of presence (and self-remembering) that will give you an entirely different experience. This is virtually an alchemical phenomenon effected by a new form of will, a new relationship to one's sense of identity, and a new understanding of the purpose of one's existence.

Once again, you are correct in your intuition that being passive to personality does in fact weaken it.

You might find it useful to read material from a different stream as you seek to apply the teachings of Nicoll. St. Augustine's Confessions come to mind. The mystics were certainly focused on inner transformation. This may add a strong emotional element to the entire process.

QUESTION:
Should the transformation be seen primarily as a means of "neutralizing" negative reactions to impressions, or could it also be a way to self-remembering, little by little? In other words: Is there a connection between transformation and self-remembering?

RESPONSE:
To answer your second question first: Certainly, there is a connection between transformation and self-remembering. The latter is called "the third state of consciousness". It is already a form of transformation. Those rare moments in which we experience a transcendent state of joy, gratitude, peace, intense presence are

68

moments of self-remembering that we carry for a lifetime and which cry out to us of another quality of living. The Work is meant to make these moments more frequent and longer lasting through intentional effort, rather than by accident.

The purpose of dealing with negative emotions is to a) clean up our inner life so that b) we can use the energies precisely for experiences of higher consciousness. We thereby stop the wasting away of energy and redirect it for our aim of awakening, experience higher consciousness—in other words, self-remembering. Nothing can happen as long as we remain in the same darkened condition. One of my favorite quotes from Nicoll is: "How can you change if you remain the same?"
Overcoming our wrong work leads to the possibility of re-channeling that energy with the help of knowledge and understanding in order to create new "being".

QUESTION:
1. Could self-observation be practiced all the hours of the day, or is it better to confine it to certain hours, and leave the mind to "rest" the remaining time?

RESPONSE:
It is not possible to practice self-observation all the time. In fact, one of the critical discoveries in this effort lies precisely in seeing how often we forget to do this. This forgetting is of course falling into the natural state of Sleep in which we all live as stimulus-response machines, to use Gurdjieff's language. Remember that this primary effort of the Work is a first step that evolves with personal experience. What you are creating by this effort is: a) a point of awareness beyond your mechanical behavior, and, b) a gathering of more objective information about yourself. This kind of self-knowledge is a cornerstone to spiritual evolution, as was stated by Socrates and all the great sages of humanity. Since we live primarily in illusions and self delusions, it is necessary to face the reality of how much of our "pictures" of ourselves are imaginary. As the Hindus say, we live in "Maya" (illusion) and it is this ignorance that keeps us asleep to our true potential and birthright.

Regarding this new point of awareness which is the birth of Observing I, this is the baby step of a new state of being, one that will lead to the ability to live in the presence with detachment, peace, independence of outer circumstances, freedom from distorted and imitated habits.

QUESTION:

. . . and have found it rewarding in many ways (for instance a more relaxed state of the body, less of mechanical reactions like irritation, anger and worry . A problem is of course that mechanical reactions now and then takes over at the cost of Observing I, but sooner or later the latter "wakes up", and starts to work again, noticing what happened in the "absence". In short: Is this an adequate way to work?

RESPONSE:

Certainly, there must be balance. And we must learn to "bargain" with the powerful aspects of our nature (Gurdjieff said that we were three-brained beings—composed of the Intellectual Center, the Emotional Center and the Instinctive Center). The latter he named in French "le patron" (the boss) and we often must appease it so that it does not come back at us with a vengeance.

However, it is important to recognize that when we are not attempting to "be present" (which means aware of ourselves to some extent), then our life is either wasting away or running out of control. In the long run, self-observation leads us to living in a state of relaxation because we are less identified (a very key concept) and therefore released from the constant flow of thoughts, feelings, and imagination that poison our existence. Therefore, the aim is to find in this initial exercise a new joy of being in the moment that was very rare before this effort of becoming more conscious and only came to us by accident.

QUESTION:

2. When (Observing) I is separating and detaching from reactions to impressions, by saying for instance "This is not me - I", is it correct to apply that to all impressions, and reactions to impressions, independently if they are "negative" or "positive"? In other words: Should Observing I in that way exclude everything that belongs to

the many I's and Me's of personal self?

RESPONSE:
The important factor here is to become free from the wrong work of your mechanics. If the body is hungry, self-observation will recognize that fact and deal with it without "becoming the hunger". What this effort leads to in the long run is "purity of heart", sensitive of conscience, and discernment. This last word means that you will be able to disentangle your sense of self from passing thoughts that randomly enter your mind and emotions. This is a very significant development on the spiritual journey. But in order to achieve these skills of perception, you have to have a different relationship with what is occurring in your inner world. Therefore self-observation simply sees. By that seeing, you are already disengaged to some extent from what you are witnessing. It does not mean that everything is alien to who you are, but that you are not victimized by all that occurs in your psychology.

QUESTION:
What is really the place of meditation in the Work? How did Gurdjieff and Ouspensky view it? Could the techniques of self-observation in the Work - inner separation, non-identification, and passivity to personality, etc., be practiced in meditation?

RESPONSE:
Gurdjieff had his students start the day at the Prieure where he taught for some years with 45 minutes of silence. This was not a time to practice self-observation—that is for use in the "heat of the battle" when there are mechanics at work to be discovered.
Meditation helps to quiet the mind, body, soul. This is valuable for anyone. Have you seen the material we translated about the practice of meditation?
This would be a way to clear the ground a bit and give you additional force to avoid immediate identification first thing in the morning.
By the way, you should expect strong resistance because our False Personality knows that the Work is out to destroy it. This is why you must use the intellect and as much understanding as possible in

dealing with yourself. Faith in something higher than oneself is crucial.

VI
A NEW RHYTHM OF LIFE

In slowing down, you will find healing. None of us can get anywhere in terms of breaking out of the vicious cycle of being what we are or finding something sacred and wonderful about life if we don't create some opportunity internally to slow down, to go deeper into our own center where we will find the great mysteries of life. Here is where this teaching becomes extremely useful because it helps you get into that center while you are in the hurricane. Not just in quiet meditation at dawn, but in the traffic or at the office. When you carry inner observation with you, you are laying the groundwork for building an inner sanctuary within all circumstances. This ultimately means consciousness of the Divine in the midst of the chaos that all of our lives have. To one degree or another we are all in the same boat, and we all have the same possibility of finding an oasis. We are not meant to be these frazzled, confused, unhappy people. This is what the religions try to give us, but they often give it to us as "just believe this and that will do it."

This Work sidesteps all of the theological knots and confusion and gets down to who you are and how you operate and tells you what you can do about it. So what does this lead to and make this strange Work worthwhile.

We have no control over these brief higher states, how long they last or when they come. The saints will state the same from their contemplative experiences. They cannot make the sacred, the numinous be present. They can only wait for it. This waiting is a special psychological state which may be easier to do in a monastic cell at a different rhythm. But how do we wait on God, how do we become receptive in our lives to something more? Again, this is what this Work is about. If you can't control the higher state -- either when it comes or how long it lasts -- what can you do? How can you make it happen? All of this Work leads to maximizing the higher states that occur to us more regularly and lasting longer. To do this, we have to set our psychological house in order. We have to stop the massive hemorrhaging of our energy and of our mindset which takes place from the moment we get up to the minute we go to sleep. If within fifteen minutes after you get out of bed, you are wired or all caught up in something, you are done for. It is going to be a momentum lasting, most likely, all day long.

All of the religious, philosophical, esoteric people of the world say that you must get to a point where many times during the say, you can have a moment of stopping and recentering so that you are not just carried along by what is happening. Muslim do this, at least theoretically. If your day has a lot of frustration in it and a lot of busy work, where are you going to find room for the peace that passes understanding, for the state of mind that is receptive to the more mysterious aspects of life, to the higher Self which is not just an office worker and has a right to just be.

PART II

APPLICATIONS AND CONNECTIONS

"You must pray with your whole presence and with all three centers concentrated on the same thing. You must pray with your head, your feeling, your sensation...Afterwards, you will speak differently, you will be able to help someone, not with gifts of money or food -- next to this that's cheap -- but you will be able to help him with a real wish, a real relationship, with all the force of your I AM."

G.I. Gurdjieff, in a transcript from one of his last meetings, quoted in *Gurdjieff: Reflections on the Man and his Teachings,* edited by Jacob Needleman and George Baker

1

A New Perspective

In his book *A Different Christianity* Robin brings together for the first time -- in a stunning feat of metaphysical detective work -- the mystical teachings of early Christianity with Perennial esoteric wisdom. Here we find the thread that connects Gurdjieff and the hermits of third century Egypt, John of the Cross and Isaac the Syrian, *Hesychia* (inner tranquility) and Hindu *Advaita* (non-duality), ancient monastic spiritual practices and the holistic insights of the New Age. Author Robin Amis, a long-time teacher of the path to conscious evolution, offers a world desperate for inner transformation a treasure map to the house of the soul.

This book has the potential of revolutionizing contemporary assumptions about the Christian Faith and providing the missing links in esoteric teachings such as the Fourth Way. A masterwork of synergy and understanding, *A Different Christianity* is potent food for the serious reader's transformation of being.

The author's fundamental thesis is that Christianity possesses an inner tradition that has never been common knowledge in the Western world. This Esoteric Christianity was once known as the "Royal Way" and has barely survived except in places like the monasticism of the Eastern Church. The author claims that we can find traces, in some of the great spiritual texts, of teachings that deal with experiential transformation and go back to the first centuries of the Church. But from the time of Clement of Alexandria, one of the beacons of this inner wisdom, various factors have caused the "unplanned but effective censorship" and forgetfulness of these powerful ideas. Amis clearly differentiates between Christian gnosis and the gnostic sects. *Gnosis*, as used here, is a special kind of inner knowledge handed down unwritten by the Apostles and is quite different from the mythologies of the later sects.

Along with his scholarly research, Mr. Amis shares his own personal experiences in seeking out this lost teaching. He details his visits to Mount Athos where this spiritual wisdom has been passed on for a thousand years. He describes the island as a "place that can help one discover the eternal within oneself." His conversation with a *pneumaticos* (spiritual hermit) is particularly striking for he is given a message to the West: "You English have served man very well with your intellect...Now you should do another work: to understand and to tell the world of the inner truth, the truth of the heart." This book is the fulfillment of that extraordinary charge.

In another sharing of his experience on the Greek peninsula, the author describes the psychosomatic impact of liturgy: "I began to understand what was really possible for a human being." Later, under a pine tree overlooking the Aegean Sea, he encounters the inward stillness that is the apex of hesychast wisdom. "Within that stillness emerged a presence I can never describe." Amis proceeds to detail the psychological phenomenon of spiritual awakening as expressed by the inner tradition. He writes extensively of the Greek philosophical concept of the *nous* which he understands as the cognitive power at the center of our being. The author provides numerous quotes from sources of wisdom rarely found in the West, including the second century work of Clement and of the nineteenth century Russian *staretz* (spiritual teacher) Theophan the Recluse. Such teachings may be found in classic texts like *The Philokalia* and *Unseen Warfare* but virtually no one has integrated them with modern esoteric thought.

The process of awakening presented here includes inner separation, the watch of the heart, metanoia, remembrance of God, magnetic center, self-observation, dispassion, and *theosis* (God- realization) and other foundational methods. Part of the discipline of the Royal Way (the inner tradition of the early Church) is to perceive without prejudgment, an effort that requires the development of transcendent self-control. This process is one that does not go against one's nature -- as happens with misguided asceticism -- but rather uncovers one's true nature.

A key idea in this teaching is *Diakrisis* (discrimination) which enables us to change our attitudes to ourselves and to detect influences acting upon our minds. "Effective *diakrisis* is nothing more than clear psychological perception...given form by real knowledge of our human nature." This implies the development of profound and brutally honest self-knowledge, a critical step to spiritual evolution. Here we find direct links between the ancient wisdom of the early Fathers of the desert and the contemporary teachings of Gurdjieff and Ouspensky, known as the Fourth Way, dealing with inner work on oneself. These efforts contribute to the goal of esotericism which Amis defines as "inner autonomy of spirit."

Bringing together the insights of the past with modern esoteric science, the author offers an outline of this path of inner transformation:

1. Discrimination -- change of mind --a renunciation of belief in ordinary worldly goals.

2. Detachment -- change of heart -- a loss of conviction in our view of the world. 3. Awakening -- renewal of intelligence (*nous*) -- new kind of knowledge.

4. Union -- complete absorption in the divine.

Through this inner effort, we find ourselves on the Way. But this Way has to be reached before we can travel on it. Amis writes of the process of "dipping" (as cloth is dipped in dye) which leads to cumulative change in the direction of our lives. This change in what we want out of life forms a "track" that leads to the next stage which is known as the "ladder." These ideas were first unearthed from the past by Boris Mouravieff whose extraordinary trilogy, *Gnosis: Study and Commentaries on the Esoteric Teachings of Eastern Orthodoxy* were co-translated and published by Amis in the last several years.

One of the most important contributions of this work comes with the author's presentation of noetic prayer. This "method" is at the heart of the Royal Way. But it little resembles what usually passes for prayer. "Prayer as it progresses depends more on a relinquishing of control than on its intensification...Directed prayer involves what one can only call a kind of effortless effort."

This approach comes out of the hesychia wisdom which deals with the deep stillness of the heart. Amis tells us that over activity is a symptom of the absence of true prayer of the heart. Noetic prayer is then a tool and a gateway for inner transformation. However, before we can reach this depth of prayer, there is need for *nepsis* or watchfulness which is the awareness and control of our inner mental and emotional activity.

Similar to Buddhist mindfulness and certainly equivalent to Gurdjieff's self-observation and self-remembering, this technique is fundamental to authentic spiritual awakening. Both watchfulness and prayer are meant to move from practices to a state of being in which they merge into a higher quality of consciousness once called "ceaseless prayer." Amis points out with exquisite insight that we generally confuse control with attention. He notes that these phenomena are connected only by the fact that attention is necessary before we can control something. Yet prayer requires attention without control. The surfacing of these powerful ideas reveals the dynamic of being in the world but not of it. The author names it *freedom from psychological captivity.*

The practice of perceiving without reacting leads to an alternative worldview. This in turn allows us to register more subtle, non-sensory experiences that open the way to spiritual consciousness. Here is found the source of gnosis coming from real being that leads to transformation of human character. Amis writes that "the true higher knowledge, the heart of knowledge, is the emotional knowledge that is born of direct experience rooted in love."

The Royal Way, then, is the narrow way of the gospel which is walked with a conscious awareness and discrimination of influences acting upon us. This effort generates the motivating force for metanoia (change of mind) leading to purity of heart which is the very basis of Christian psychological development. Amis here reveals the stream of inner tradition from which Gurdjieff's teachings arose. The outward difference is due to Gurdjieff's use of a simpler form designed for a secular world and with additions borrowed from other inner traditions. This method is not one of obedience but of personal choice originating from a certain state of mind (sometimes called conscience) and resulting in a change of consciousness described as "waking up."

In a striking anecdote resulting from his years of research, Amis informs us that, shortly before his death, Gurdjieff arranged for a group to travel to Mount Athos in an effort to re- establish contact with the tradition. The author claims that making the connection with this ancient teaching virtually lost to the world completes the incomplete system of inner work which Ouspensky called "fragments of an unknown teaching." Such a reconstitution then lead to results of a new kind. This book offers us the missing pieces that can revive a teaching of great power which has the potential of revitalizing the spirituality of the Western world.

2

Recovering our True Self:

The Journey Out of Our Negative States

Down through the centuries, spiritual teachers of all traditions have differentiated between our mundane, invented personality so filled with stress, and our true identity characterized by serenity, constancy, and wisdom. They urge us to discover our inner depths and that vaster Self which enables right action in the world. Everyone of us is meant to live with joy and compassionate outreach to the people around us. We are designed to be masters of our selves, capable of overcoming all the difficulties of life. This is our birthright, but in order to experience it, we must recognize how far we are from living in this manner, why this is so, and what efforts we must make to live in such a way. This new awareness and these efforts are the process that leads us out of our negative emotional habits in order to enter into the depths of our spiritual nature.

To recover from our ingrained habits and our subconscious imitations of parents and peers is truly spiritual warfare. It is the narrow way that few want to travel as it requires going against the grain of our own behavior. It is making the hard choices rather than taking the easy way as we always have. This process takes place in the trenches of our most ordinary interactions with the world. Authentic spiritual development takes place in that moment of irritation, that moment of unkindness, that moment of selfishness that we encounter the heat of the battle. This inner battle determines who we are and how we live this life during our brief journey through time.

Here then are some specific methods for recovering from those toxic habits:

The first and most fundamental effort is *the objective study of ourselves.* Why? Because nothing real can take place until we know what we are dealing with. We cannot take for granted that we know how or why we function the way we do. If you want to operate a computer, you have to learn the software. Human beings are complex software indeed and are rarely user friendly. So try *observing yourself* from a completely neutral standpoint. Do not judge what you see. Just see it. Observe your reactions, your attitudes, your moods and the many aspects of yourself that take charge from moment to moment. If you do this with sincerity and courage, not justifying every action and passing thought, you will begin to see yourself more objectively and initiate the *awareness of the Observing Self* who will be the key to your recovery.

This simple effort begins the process of creating a space within you that is not completely hypnotized by external events. Though you still react to external circumstances through ingrained habit, there is now this sliver of your Self that is not pulled out of you. A new space of inner freedom is being created along with a new sense of a deeper identity than the surface personality.

Another critical aspect of this observation is the study of our negative states. You will be amazed at how much of our time is spent under the dominance of these dark moods and thoughts. You will catch yourself grumbling about other people, feeling dejected over this or that event, complaining about the weather, resenting something somebody said. Nothing healthy can grow under the constant downpour of this acid rain within you. Eventually, you will discover that you can free yourself from such unpleasant behavior and states of mind. Step one is to turn off the leaking faucet: *stop expressing negative emotions.*

This effort is the beginning of separating yourself from them. You don't have to accept living in those dark states. You are not them. They are bad habits acquired over a lifetime. If you want healing and joy in your life, you must stop the momentum of negativity. One of the important things to observe about negative states is how much energy they take away from us. If you are aware of yourself before and after a moment of rage, you will see very clearly how much energy has been lost in that brief moment. We only have so much energy available to us each day, and we can use it to be healed and renewed, or we can squander it thoughtlessly.

So notice your thoughts before they plant themselves in your feelings and eventually manifest in your actions. Anger at a colleague or spouse can be caught before it has caused internal and external damage. In that more rational, detached place before the feeling has caught you by the throat, you can notice why you are angry. What is it in you that is reacting that way? What is it in your colleague that has caused his or her behavior which is so disturbing? Anger can then turn into compassion, or at least into a new insight about yourself or another.

After self-observation and separation from negative states comes the next all-important practice: *becoming present to the moment.* Experience the moment as it is, for what it is. Becoming present grounds you in reality here and now and takes you out of the tempests of imagination and inner talking that fill the mind with so much noise. Become present not only to your surroundings, but to your body. Relax the tensions that you haven't even noticed before: In the shoulders, in the jaws, in the stomach. Begin to experience the revitalizing peace of being alive in this moment. Those of you familiar with meditation know how helpful it is to regulate one's breathing in order to center oneself. Just breathing in and out slowly to ease the inner tensions is a powerful tool for nourishing your spirit in the moment. Learn to sit quietly for awhile. This is no luxury or idle behavior. We are so wracked with stress and worry that we cannot recover enough to get back in touch with ourselves until we are released from the grip of our anxieties. We rob ourselves of the very joy of living when we let ourselves fall into endless worry and nervous tension. Take time to let go of all that.

This daily effort teaches us to stop or at least to step back from the constant flow of thoughts that creates reality for us. This means that most of our worrying and anxious considerations fall by the wayside and we are able to rise above the clouds of our immediate concerns to the larger picture of our existence as a whole. Sometimes, however, the flood of thoughts refuses to slow no matter what we do. Our nerves are so frayed that we cannot achieve the simple peace of looking out the window and enjoying the view without anything coming to mind. That's when you might employ the *stop exercise*. In the midst of a thought or daydream, tell yourself to stop and abruptly cut short what is going on in your mind. Then relax your body and look around you, just seeing what is there. Take a vacation from the inner turmoil.

So our daily practice for recovering from a life polluted with negative emotional habits includes: *objective observation of our selves, separation from negative states, quieting the mind, and becoming present to the moment.* You will notice how these practices begin to take us out of our usual nervous tension and keep us from mindlessly responding to everything around us by turning a portion of our attention inward and by expanding our perspective in the moment. We then become more than our self-centered, habitual mass of reactions.

If you apply these techniques regularly, you will soon find yourself living more frequently in that space of peace, of centeredness, of recovery from being victims of automatic reactions. Then you will find that you become capable of a serenity and acceptance of what is, of a surrender of selfishness that empowers you to help others as well as yourself.

Such a journey of emotional and psychological recovery offers us a new spiritual empowerment which enables us to accept life as it comes, even with all its complications and the capacity to act rightly in any given situation. This developing inner power creates a free human being who is no longer entangled in his or her selfishness and constant stream of fears and desires. Such a person can journey through life in peace, with wisdom and compassion. Such a person makes the world a better place.

3

Our Spiritual Habitat

Spiritual teachers have described their experience of the habitat or environment of the soul as *cosmic consciousness, peak experience, the peace that passes all understanding, the inner light, becoming transparent to the divine.* Whatever words are used to describe it, the result of encountering this inner depth is always the same -- it enables entrance into a vaster identity and wisdom which enables right action to be manifested in the world.

We are each meant to live with serenity, joy, and compassionate outreach to the world around us. We are meant to be masters of our selves, capable of overcoming all the difficulties of life. This is our birthright, but in order to experience it we must recognize how far we are from living in this manner, why this is so, and what efforts we must make to live in such a way. This new awareness and these efforts are the process that leads us into the depths of our spiritual nature, our true habitat.

The first step along this path is to notice that we live in *different states of consciousness.* This is not as obvious as it sounds. I am not referring here to moments of happiness in contrast to times of depression, but to *a state of being* that puts us in touch with a deeper reality. Perhaps you have had moments of experiencing such a liberation that comes from these higher states of being. Moments of great joy, or gratitude for being alive, or while standing before a scene of great beauty. Moments when our awareness is lifted beyond the knots and tensions of our worries and concerns and we are free to enjoy the experience of being fully grounded in the present and happy to be alive.

These are higher states of consciousness that open onto new horizons of understanding and wisdom. You may have had such experiences as children when we were less weighed down by the things that now preoccupy us. You may even have fallen for the illusion that those times of bliss and wonder are gone forever along with the other delights of childhood. But that is not the case. We are meant to dwell permanently in this habitat of the soul where higher consciousness dwells. It is possible to taste and live this joy and freedom, this inner awakening, even during rush hour, even at the office, even when circumstances around you are difficult.

In order to identify our true habitat, let's take a look at what it is *not*: our everyday state of consciousness. Teachings on this subject describe our usual condition of consciousness as a *state of sleep*. Though we all believe that we are fully conscious in every moment of our lives, the fact is that most of our existence is spent "on automatic." We are stimulus-response organisms: something happens to us and we react. We think we choose how we behave, but most often we are simply one giant knee-jerk reaction to whatever comes our way: -- your child disobeys you and you get angry -- you spill a drink on yourself and you're embarrassed -- the red light lasts too long and you're impatient the list is endless, from morning till night. It's the world of stress, of ups and downs, of good days and bad days, of insecurity, inconsistency, unreliability. It's the world we know so well.

If you think the word "sleep" is a strange way to describe our condition, just think back on the last time you observed someone watching television. The vacant stare, the loose jaw...we are virtually hypnotized by life around us, drawn out of ourselves and no more able to make choices than when we are in the middle of a dream. Things happen and we respond

according to our programming. It is all consuming. Our first
obstacle is therefore our wrong perspective on our lives. We
take ourselves for granted. We believe that we are one and
the same person all the time. But take a closer look and dare
to be honest with yourself. When you're really hungry, the
you that is hungry is in charge in charge. When you're
irritable, the you that is irritated is the boss. When you're
tired, when you're excited, when you're mad, each mood and
desire is in control. Where is the unity of oneself in all that?
Again, we function in a stimulus-response manner that takes
away our capacity to be unified as individuals. *We cannot count
on ourselves to be the same person from one moment to the next.* The
person who decides the night before to get up early in the
morning is not the one who has to turn off the alarm and roll
out of bed. That person has a very different idea of what he
or she wants to do.
To make matters worse, each of these impulses that claims to
be the whole person is separated by blinders. They do not
know each other. When we are our happy-go-lucky selves, we
don't remember the mean-tempered one. Our condition of
multiplicity is further complicated by the fact that we live so
much of our life in imagination. Consider how much time is
spent worrying about the future, or fretting over the past.
Think of all the daydreaming that goes on in your head. And
look at how we bounce from one thought to the next without
any intentionality or purpose: someone mentions a word (like
blue) and our mind takes us off on a tangent that gets more
and more tangled until we no longer have any idea how we
got to a certain mood or idea. So in our ordinary state of
consciousness we are made of many disconnected selves, we
are pulled to and fro by imagination and unintentional
thoughts and yet we think we are in full control of ourselves.

Now we come to an even more fundamentally problem: our
essential nature, that which we truly are -- the sensitivities, the
gifts, the inclinations we were born with -- is generally
repressed at an early stage of our life. As we encounter the
world around us, the essence of who we are becomes covered
over by the development of our personality. Here again, we

take for granted that our personality is who we genuinely are. But our personality is rarely related to our essence and our natural inclinations. Throughout our pre-teen, adolescent, and early adulthood years we have, both consciously and unconsciously, built up defense mechanisms to survive the pain of dealing with life. We have developed masks to protect ourselves or to manipulate others. Furthermore, we have absorbed into our idea of ourselves the images that our culture tells us are the acceptable way of being a man or a woman.

We have accumulated the imitations or our parents, our peers and our environment. In a word, we have covered over our essential nature to such an extent that we have to virtually undertake an archeological exploration in order to rediscover ourselves. In order to find the habitat of our soul, in order to live right, we have to be aligned with our real self. But there are powerful forces in the way. The greatest among them is negativity in all its forms: irritation, anger, impatience, depression, hatred, vengeance, jealousy, envy, and resentment. These are all poisons within us that cause us so much unnecessary suffering and use up so much of our energy, our life-force. We don't have to live like that! Even though it seems that everyone around us indulges in these negative forms of behavior, they are not the only way to live. Imagine how different your life would be without the constant stress of these wretched feelings.

But that entails dealing with our greatest foe: our vanity. Vanity is not merely primping in the mirror. It causes us to spend much of our life in self-interested activity, in thinking about ourselves, in having to be right, in asserting ourselves over others, in stubbing our pride over this or that. Vanity causes us to have a false idea of ourselves, a false sense of self-importance along with a perverse distortion of our attention through self-absorption. Everything becomes "me, me, me." So much grief and misery comes from this petty self-centeredness that disfigures our humanity. We are our own greatest source of suffering as long as we live in this state of sleep that is ruled by automatic behavior, a self-centered focus, negative emotions, multiple selves vying for control, and misperceptions of who we truly are.

So what is the true habitat of the soul? Clearly it is not merely a place. It is the life-force beyond our mistaken notion of ourselves that is seeking to come through us and accomplish its work of goodness in the world. It is that mysterious "presence" that can overcome solitude, meaninglessness, and despair. Moreover, not only is it always there -- deep within -- but it is seeking us more than we are seeking it. This habitat is common to us all. We are not merely separate, disconnected life forms as the senses suggest. We are all connected and rooted in the deeper life that brought us into being. This habitat is our source of hope and sanity in a world of chaos. We are a part of the greater life form which all a things come, and with that awareness, we discover our real importance and purpose in the world. To become connected to inner spiritual home, which is so intimate to us and yet so much more than we are, is to come in contact with the very mystery of our existence. And the more we enter our true habitat at the center of our being, the more we are made whole and capable of caring for others.

4

The Art of Getting Along With Others

Most of us have noticed over the years that getting along with others doesn't always come easy. Perhaps you have seen recurring patterns, instantaneously liking or disliking someone for no apparent reason, being attracted or repulsed by people you don't know anything about. Getting along with other people is in many ways an art form, or more specifically a science, that each one of us needs to try to master as best as we can.

One of the philosophers of our age teaches that a part of our maturing process as human beings is to "*learn to bear the unpleasant manifestations of others.*" We can all agree that accomplishing that aim is an epic task. It helps to know that others have to learn to bear our own unpleasant manifestations and perhaps we can be a little more understanding of why people act the way they do. Imagine how different life would be if people didn't rub you the wrong way, didn't offend you, didn't cause you embarrassment, and all that long list of reactions that makes our days so difficult.

In learning this science of dealing with all kinds of people, we find that human beings are more alike than not. There are only so many "*types*" of people, even though each individual is unique. If you come to know your type, you might better understand why another "type" is problematic. Such knowledge can lead to a new perspective, freed from judgment and rejection. For instance, we can see that there are positive types and negative types – people who see the glass half full and others who see it as half empty. It is not right or wrong, but merely how their perceiving apparatus functions.

Another common denominator that can be found among all people are active types and passive types. Again, there is no good or bad attached to these features. We all know the sort of person who is a "bull in a china shop" and seems to break things every time he or she turns around. Sometimes they don't even know they are behaving this way. They are just being who they are. We can observe that others are quiet or withdrawn, not because they are antisocial but because their nature is set to a "different volume". In all these differences we find positive attributes. The bull can also be a person of great loyalty and courage. The quiet person can kind and thoughtful.

It boils down to learning how to see people with understanding rather than judgment or knee-jerk reaction. One of the ways we reach that kind of compassion and acceptance is to see ourselves in others and others in ourselves. Regardless of our differences, we share much in common. We all need to be loved, we all need to be heard, we all need to be accepted and forgiven. What a different place the world would be if more of us developed this ability to see people with eyes that do not condemn.

Down through the centuries, there have been studies of the different types of people we see around us in an effort to understand why we act as we do. From the influence of cosmic forces to the functioning of our endocrine system, fascinating insights have evolved regarding human behavior (think of the red-headed warrior type constantly fired up by his adrenalins). Even though each of us is a one of a kind individual, it is easy to see that our physical traits are duplicated in others. If you have traveled the world, you have seen faces and body shapes that look remarkably alike on different sides of the globe.

The practice of this art of getting along with others includes recognizing that, while being unique individuals, everyone has particular "hardware" with which we come into the world. Along with or sizes and shapes, we are also wired with certain psychological traits. Some people are driven by the need for dominance, others by fear, others by vanity, and until we become more aware of ourselves, we often do not know what it is that motivates us or generates our actions and reactions. If we are honest with ourselves, we can clearly see that we tend to always respond in the same way to certain situations. We might even be able to admit that we often function like stimulus-response mechanisms to the circumstances and people in our lives, predictable and repetitive.

One of the spiritual purposes for our existence is to activate our free will so that we can choose to not react in the same old way but rather for the sake of the greater good. That takes real discipline, powerful self-control, and a determined desire to manifest to best part of ourselves. It takes mature insight to realize that we are not merely our reactions. We are more than our personality. So much of who we think we are is built up from parental imitation, cultural influence, imagination and illusion. If we dare to dig through all that we just might find our true Self, the person we were in childhood, the individual buried deep within behind the scars and the fears and the pain. Our true purpose is to realize that we have lost sight of ourselves and need to make the journey home to our true identity, just like the parable of the prodigal son instructs us to do. Then we no longer need to have power over others, to prove ourselves, to hide our insecurities, to depend on the opinions of other people. We will have entered into freedom, first and foremost from our automatic behavior which belongs to our type and to our upbringing, but not to our spirit.

Such development empowers us to choose to behave and react in new ways for the sake of a higher good. To disengage from our familiar forms of behavior frees us from being puppets on a string, always responding the same way to external stimuli. In that state of greater awareness and understanding, we enter into our true destiny and our true happiness. We are then no longer merely our type but rather children of God bringing goodness and a positive influence into our world.

PART III

PERENNIAL ROOTS

"He on whom your attention rests is your neighbor; he also will die...If you acquire data always to realize the inevitability of their death and your own death, you will have a feeling of pity for others, and be just toward them...From realizing the significance of your neighbor when your attention rests on him, that he will die, pity for him and compassion toward him will arise in you, and finally you will love him; also, by doing this constantly, real faith, conscious faith, will arise in some part of you and spread to other parts, and you will have the possibility of knowing real happiness."

Gurdjieff:: Reflections on the Man and his Teachings, edited by Jacob Needleman and George Baker

Introduction

There are traces of a universal wisdom with the power to transform human consciousness in all the great teachings of humanity. The radiance of the individuals who find and apply these timeless teachings are a blessing to others for centuries after their time on earth. A common thread can be uncovered in the processes and goals of such powerful ideas. In the following chapters, the reader will note that, from the most unexpected and disparate sources, one can find that thread and its resultant impact on the human psyche.

Whether in esoteric groups gathered to study and sustain this spiritual knowledge, or in ancient Hebrew symbolism and numerology, or at the heights of medieval Christian mysticism, the commonalities reveal a teaching that transcends cultures, religions, and time itself.

It is out of that unfathomable and mysterious well of wisdom stretching across the ages that the teaching known in this time as "the Fourth Way" arises. It does not belong to particular people, nor to specific teachers. It is a trace of divine teaching that awakens the human soul to its highest potential. Any attempt to formalize it, dogmatize it, and box it in a particular tradition is to destroy it.

1

THE MYSTERY OF THE ESSENES

Information concerning the Essenes, prior to the Dead Sea Scrolls, comes to us from two ancient scholars, both of whom were contemporaries of the first century Essenes: Josephus Flavius and Philo of Alexandria.

Josephus, born at Jerusalem in 37 A.D., was the greatest historian of the Jews in that period. Philo was the greatest Jewish philosopher of that period. Both men had personal knowledge of the ancient Essenes.

Both scholars make clear that the Essenian roots are incredibly ancient. Josephus declares that the Essenes have existed "from time immemorial" and "countless generations". Philo agrees, calling the Essenes "the most ancient of all the initiates" with a "teaching perpetuated through an immense space of ages".

Records of the Essene way of life have come down to us from writings of their contemporaries. Pliny, the Roman naturalist, and others spoke of them variously as "a race by themselves, more remarkable than any other in the world," "the oldest of the initiates, receiving their teaching from Central Asia," "teaching perpetuated through an immense space of ages," "constant and unalterable holiness."

Josephus and Philo -- as well as several other ancient writers including Pliny the Elder -- are in consensus on two points in regard to the origin of the Essenes:

1.   Their origin is lost in pre-history with certain ancient legends linking them with Enoch;

2.   There was a major remanifestation of the Essenes by Moses at Mount Sinai.

Enoch lived many centuries before Moses. In the fifth chapter of the Book of Genesis (the first book of the bible), Enoch is described as "the seventh from Adam" -- which means he was born seven generations after Adam. Since seven, in Essene numerology, is the number of perfection, it is no mere coincidence that Enoch represents the seventh generation of humanity: he represents perfected humanity.

While much of the Enochian legend cited above is found only in Essene Kaballah texts, it stems directly from the Bible: Genesis chapter five verse twenty-four: *"Enoch walked with God; and he was not, for God took him."*

The fact that Enoch was considered the "founder" or "initiator" of the Essenes can even be seen in his name; the word "Enoch" means in Hebrew: "founder", "initiator", "centralizer".

ORIGINS

The Essenes have their roots in Egypt during the late Eighteenth Dynasty. These were equated with purity, and the polarity of light, as opposed to darkness. It is unclear as to exactly when the Brotherhood was formed, but many of the rules and regulations appear to be have been formulated by Pharaoh Tuthmose III.

The aim of the Brotherhood was to preserve the great knowledge attained by the wisest of Egypt. It could in some ways be seen as a school of philosophy. Students from around the globe travelled to Egypt in order to study under their directorship.

The name Essene is thought to derive from the Egyptian kashai, meaning secret. There is also a Jewish word chshai, meaning secret, or silent, which would naturally translate as Essene. The Jewish historian, Josephus found that the Egyptian symbols for light and truth were represented in the word chosen, which in Greek also translates to Essen, leading to speculation that the Essenes may in fact be the chosen ones mentioned in The Bible. Chosen is derived from the Aramaic asaya, meaning physician, or healer, a role for which the Essenes were well known and highly respected. The Greek word for physician is of course, therapeautae, and for this reason, The Brothers were known as Therapeutae within the Greek speaking world.

The Essenes referred to themselves as essania, meaning 'Sons of the Sun'. This may help to explain why one of the most important movers in the early formation of the Brotherhood, the so called heretic Pharaoh, Akhenaten (Tuthmose III Great, Great Grandson) abandoned the old Gods in favour of the Aten, as represented by the solar disc.

The best known of the Essene communities was undoubtedly Qumran near the Dead Sea, where the famous Dead Sea Scrolls were found in 1947. So far over 800 scrolls, have been found, ranging from hymns and prayers, community rules, and copies of various Biblical texts. The most unusual of these, the Copper Scroll was found in cave number three, and appeared to be an ancient treasure map, listing 64 different caches, much of which are believed to have come from the Temple of Jerusalem. Many of the sites mentioned in the scroll have since been excavated, but no treasure has been found.

Scholar and author Robert Feather believes that the reason for this is that archaeologists have been looking in the wrong place, or to be more precise, the wrong country. He believes that the treasure is not to be found in Israel, but rather in Egypt, at the ruins of Amarna, Akhenaten's capital city. Moses is said to have been a pupil of Akhenaten. The Essenes claimed to have received much of their esoteric teachings from Moses.

When the Copper Scroll was finally translated by John Allegro, in addition to Hebrew writing, it was also found to contain 14 letters from the Greek alphabet, interspersed throughout the text. When Feather looked at these in more detail, he found that when put together, they spelt the Greek name for Akhenaten.

THE UNIVERSAL TEACHING OF AKHENATEN

One of the most critical links between various religions, revealing that the truth they teach is the same, is seen in the little known fact that Hebrew spiritual knowledge originated in the teachings of ancient Egypt. This assertion would tie the teachings of the Torah to the source of all the primary streams of esoteric knowledge available to humanity. Egypt was the location of the great library of Alexandria and the center of esoteric schools that attracted the likes of Plato.

This oneness of Truth is a most compelling idea in our day and age when the reality of the global community and our interconnection across all nations and cultures is an obvious daily event. It carries the seeds of reconciliation, understanding and peace for our tormented world. Our work is to find the keys to the meaning of these ancient teachings that reveal the universal truth which sets us free.

The sacred wisdom of the Hebrews clearly dates back to more ancient sources. This connection is no longer merely the opinion of metaphysical organizations, but proven by modern biblical scholarship to be true. A classic example of this phenomenon is found in Psalm 104, the famous "pearl of the Psalter." Scholars point out that, despite its parallels with Genesis 1, the psalm does not show dependence on the story of creation. It excels Genesis 1 in richness of imagination and is an older version dating from the time when the sagas of Genesis and Exodus were still in the process of flux and growth, not having as yet received their fixed literary form.

Scholars tell us that Psalm 104 is not an original composition by a Hebrew psalmist but is derived from and owes its magnificent spirit to the Hymn to the Sun attributed to Pharaoh Ikhnaton (Amenhotep IV, 1375-1358 B.C.). The noted Egyptologist Hugo Gressmann observed that, in their ideas about God and the intimate relationship that human beings may cultivate with their Creator, the Egyptians of the Eighteenth and Nineteenth Dynasties were far in advance of the Hebrews of the early monarchical period. Such ideas did not prevail to any extent until the latter half of the eighth century B.C., in the time of Amos, Isaiah and Hezekiah. The opportunity for becoming acquainted with Egyptian thought and literature was never lacking in Israel. The two countries had commercial and political ties, and maintained friendly relations down to 586 B.C. when the Hebrews were forced into exile. At the time of the Deuteronomic legislation (622 B.C.), Egyptians must have lived in considerable numbers in Israel since Deuterenomy 23:8f. states that third generation Egyptians may be admitted to the community of Yahweh.

It is well known that for nearly two millenia Egypt exercised a powerful influence over Palestine. The two cultures intermingled to such an extent that hundreds of Hebrew loan words are found in the Egyptian of the New Kingdom. King Solomon married an Egyptian princess (I Kings 9:15f.) and Moses reached a place of considerable social importance in Egypt. The scholar W.F. Albright suggests that Moses' original Torah may well have contained Egyptian elements that were later integrated with native Hebrew conceptions. Moreover, Moses introduced to his people the ancient Egyptian custom of circumcision that was practiced for at least three thousand years by the Nile dwellers.

The fact that Moses adopted as a universal distinguishing mark of the Israelites a sacred Egyptian practice is evidence that he was drawing upon his knowledge of Egyptian religion. Acts 7:22 tells us that Moses was instructed in all the wisdom of the Egyptians.

Among the major influences that can be traced back to Egyptian sources are:

1. The concept of the god who is the sole creator of everything and the formula by which his name is derived ("Who causes to be what comes into existence," which is used repeatedly in the Hymn to Amon, 15th century B.C.).
2. The concept of a single god and the establishment of a doctrine based on monotheism.
3. The recognition of a universal cosmic dominion of the deity.

Furthermore, Moses' Torah translates as "teaching," a word used exclusively in the slightly earlier system known as *shayet* (teaching) originated by Ikhnaton. Through the medium of Semitic scribes who studied Egyptian and learned their trade in the Egyptian writing-schools, many of the ideas and literary artifices contained in poems of the Eighteenth and Nineteenth Dynasties passed into Palestine. Extracts of these works may have begun to filter into Palestine even before the reign of Hezekiah, who initiated the re-copying of Egyptian poems and treatises that may well have stimulated the reform movement in Judah.

Egyptian influence penetrated Hebrew thought to such an extent that we find its influence even in the New Testament. In the myth of Isis, who was known as the mother of God, her divine child Horus is miraculously conceived and born in a stable!

The young pharaoh Ikhnaton inspired a universalism not found before in the three thousand years of Egyptian religion. He attempted to create a world religion and displaced not only the inherent nationalism in Egyptian religion, but all the gods as well in favor of a single, universal god, the Aton. Ikhnaton was the first individual we know of in history to shape his times by rejecting the sordidness of religion and the indecent wealth and lavish rituals of the temples. Some scholars suggest that he was the first person to understand rightly the meaning of divinity. For instance, Ikhnaton forbade his artists from making images of Aton on the grounds that the true God has no form.

He understood God as a life-giving intangible essence. The symbol of Aton (the sun disc from which diverging beams radiate downward, each ending in a human hand), was not worshipped. Rather, the divinity was the power that produced and sustained the energy of the sun. This Solar theology was closely identified with the development of the moral consciousness of Egypt. Aton was to be found not in battles and victories, but in flowers and trees, in all forms of life and growth. The divinity was the creative and nourishing heat of the sun that gives life to all that exists. With this depiction of the deity, Ikhnaton formulated the profound idea of God's immanence, the presence of the divine within matter and, specifically, in human form. For the first time in history, God was conceived as a formless being. Ikhnaton's god was an intangible essence, the energetic force that acted through the sun, the creator who held all things in his hands. He was both transcendent and immanent, original causation and continuous presence. The omnipresence and beneficence of the sun evolved into an understanding of Aton as a compassionate mother-father of creation. There was no mention of hatred, jealousy or wrath, of hell or of judgment of God, for Aton was called "the Lord of Love."

***

The Essenes were to all extents and purposes a very advanced, and highly evolved race of people. There were those who lived in small, enclosed settlements, and shared a communal way of life, amongst nature, where everyone was equal. Others lived in large community buildings, near cities, many of which served as inns and hospices. It is to one of these hospices, near Bethlehem that Mary, mother of Jesus was brought to give birth.

Much of their time was devoted to the study of ancient texts and various branches of the healing arts. There were also those who travelled far and wide, circulating news and information throughout the various centers that they maintained. Two principal centers were at Lake Moeris in Egypt, and in Palestine, at Engaddi, near the Dead Sea. In addition to this, for many centuries they maintained a great library and school of learning near Mount Carmel. It is here that many of their great leaders, including Jesus and John the Baptist are said to have been educated.

Like many of the ancient Gnostic groups, The Essenes believed that mankind was made up of three aspects; body, mind and emotions. The ultimate goal of the individual was the evolution, not only of him, or herself, but also with regard to the planet and universe as a whole. The body was the outer means through which this was expressed, while the mind was seen as the inner manifestation, and creator of thoughts and emotion, which the body then responded to and acted upon. Thought was therefore considered to be the highest, most powerful force in the universe, as it was seen as the instigator of both feeling and action. The Essenes therefore trained themselves to harness this power in a positive way, knowing that each thought effected the lives of everyone on the planet through the vibrations they sent out into the collective unconscious.

The Qumran community is generally believed to have been established around the year 130 BC, in order to prepare for the imminent arrival of the expected Messiah. The Royal House of David, from which the true leader of Israel was expected to come, had long since passed into the hands of outsiders, while the High Priesthood was both culturally and politically more Roman and Greek than Jewish. It therefore made sense for the Messiah to come not from these sources, but rather from amongst the Essenes.

From "The Manual of Discipline" of the Dead Sea Scrolls

"The Law was planted in the Garden of the Brotherhood to enlighten the heart of man and to make straight before him all the ways of true righteousness, a humble spirit, an even temper, a freely compassionate nature, and eternal goodness and understanding and insight, and mighty wisdom which believes in all God's works and a confident trust in His many blessings and a spirit of knowledge in all things of the Great Order, loyal feelings toward all the Children of truth, a radiant purity which loathes everything impure, a discretion regarding all the hidden things of truth and secrets of inner knowledge."

Since the archaeological discovery of the Dead Sea Scrolls in 1946, the word "Essene" has made its way around the world--often raising a lot of questions. Many people were astonished to discover that, two thousand years ago, a brotherhood of holy men and women, living together in a community, carried within themselves the seeds of Christianity and of the future western civilization.

The Essenes considered themselves the guardians of the Divine Teaching. They had in their possession a great number of very ancient manuscripts, some of them going back to the dawn of time. A large portion of the School members spent their time decoding them, translating them into several languages, and reproducing them, in order to perpetuate and preserve this advanced knowledge. They considered this work to be a sacred task.

The Essenes considered their Brotherhood-Sisterhood as the presence on earth of the Teaching of the sons and daughters of God. They were the light which shines in the darkness and which invites the darkness to change itself into light. Thus, for them, when a candidate asked to be admitted to their School, it meant that, within him, a whole process of awakening of the soul was set in motion.

The Essenes differentiated between the souls which were sleeping, drowsy, and awakened. Their task was to help, to comfort, and to relieve the sleeping souls, to try to awaken the drowsy souls, and to welcome and guide the awakened souls. Only the souls considered as awakened could be initiated into the mysteries of the Brotherhood-Sisterhood.

The Essenes considered themselves to be a separate people--not because of external signs like skin color, hair color, etc., but because of the illumination of their inner life and their knowledge of the hidden mysteries of nature unknown to other people.

***

THE CHRISTIAN CONNECTION

A number of contemporary scholars believe that, although the Essenes began as an esoteric minority sect within Judaism, they went on to become the very first "Christians," called "Essene-Nazarenes" or "Ebionites". it is quite clear that the headquarters of the entire Essene movement was Mount Carmel in Northern Israel, not Qumran in Southern Israel, and that Jesus was primarily associated with Carmel. Equally clear is the fact that the Northern Essenes in the region of Mount Carmel were called "Nazarenes". The fact that nearly every major event associated with the life of Jesus occurred in Northern Israel, is strong evidence that Jesus lived most of his life in Northern Israel. Only four events of Jesus' life occurred in Southern Israel (his birth in Bethlehem; his visit to the temple when he was 12; his baptism by John; and his final journey to Jerusalem) and each of those events is clearly described as occurring after making a long journey from his home in Northern Israel.

There is solid consensus among scholars that John the Baptist was from Qumran: the location on the Jordan river where tradition tells us John performed his baptisms is exactly where the Jordan river connects with the Dead Sea near Qumran, and everything we know about John matches up perfectly with what is known about the Qumran Essenes.

When the holy family returned from Egypt after Herod's death, we are told they settled in Nazareth. Nazareth is very near Mount Carmel, the headquarters of the entire Essene movement. However, in those days, there was no town called "Nazareth"; rather, it was simply a cooperative village of Essene "Nazarenes".

Thus, the term "Jesus of Nazareth" was originally "Jesus the Nazarene", and a "Nazarene" is a "Northern Essene" associated with Mount Carmel. Which is why in the New Testament Book of Acts, the early Christians' are referred to as "the sect of the Nazarenes."

Jesus the Nazarene has remarkable similarities with the Essene Teacher of Righteousness.

The Teacher of Righteousness is referred to in the Manual of Discipline and the Damascus Document. In the Manual of Discipline the Teacher is associated with "the time of the preparation of the Way in the wilderness" by "the teaching of the miraculous Mysteries" (cf. Isa 40:1-3 which is used in the description of John the Baptist). He is commanded to be "zealous for the Law and the day of vengeance" conjuring up explicit images of the Zealots. In John 2:27 Jesus has "zeal" and in Acts 21:20 James' followers are "zealous for the Law". In the Damascus Document the Teacher is to "walk in the Laws" until the "standing up of the Messiah of Aaron and Israel in the Last days" where standing up can be synonymous with coming, return, rising or even resurrection.

There is a reference in a scroll fragment to the "putting to death of the Righteous One". Compare this with the passage in James (5:6) which says:

Ye condemned the Righteous One; ye put him to death though he doth not resist you.

This fragment echoes other themes of, and the style of, James's epistle calling for patience and restraint. Even the language including the use of words like tongue and vipers are closely similar. Indeed the "tongue" imagery of James 3 is used to attack lying adversaries and the tongue is described by the identical, though common enough, expression, "the stumbling block", both in James and in the scroll fragment.

The above examples are beyond coincidence.

In James 2:20-24 the "Man of Emptiness" knows not that "a man was justified by his works" and "faith without works is dead", a plain contradiction of Paul's message that faith alone brings salvation, now considered to be the essence of Christianity. James is an Essene document only slightly edited by a Christian.

Other fragments also suggest that the Nasi, the Prince, of the Community was put to death, though it could be interpreted that the Nasi put someone else to death. The context is that of that revered quotation from Isaiah - "a rod shall rise from the stem of Jesse and a branch shall grow from his roots" referring to the Messiah. Elsewhere a messianic figure will overthrow the evil generation. This fragment possibly refers to a crucifixion.

The scroll scholar M. Dupont-Sommer summarizes the remarkable similarities between the Teacher of Righteousness and Jesus Christ:

- Both were martyred prophets subsequently revered by their followers as the Suffering Servant.
- Both preached penitence, poverty, humility, love of one's neighbor and chastity.
- Both prescribed observance of the Law of Moses.
- Both were the Elect of G-d and the Messiah, the redeemer of the world.
- Both were opposed by the priests, the Sadducees; were condemned and murdered.
- Both seemed to found a church whose believers thought he would return in glory, whose central rite was a sacred meal presided over by priests and whose members held goods in common and believed in brotherhood.
- Both will be the supreme judge at the Last Judgment.
- Both apparently predicted the fall of Jerusalem.

CHRISTIAN AND ESSENE COMMON FEATURES

Christianity and the Essenes sect have too many features in common for it to be chance.

- They both believe in baptism. Vermes tells us the Manual of Discipline ordained that the initiate "shall be made clean by the humble submission of his soul to all the precepts of G-d" but only after "his flesh is sprinkled with purifying water and sanctified by cleansing water".
- The earliest Christians "held all things common". The Manual of Discipline states that all shall bring their "knowledge, powers and possessions" into the Community, that they shall "eat in common and pray in common" and that a new member's property shall be "merged...to the Community".
- The early church in Jerusalem was led by the twelve Apostles (still twelve even after Judas had died showing that the Apostles were not particular persons but positions to be filled when vacant " fourteen or possibly fifteen Apostles are mentioned in the gospels) of whom Peter, James and John had special responsibility. The Community was led by a Council of 12 people, apparently with three priests having special responsibility.
- Both the Community and the first Christians were messianic: the Christians regarded Jesus as the Messiah; the Community had their "Teacher of Righteousness" with a similar history.
- Both communities also use the same phraseology. Jesus said:
- "blessed are the meek for they shall inherit the earth", an exact expression of the Community's beliefs about itself for they called themselves "the Poor" and "the Meek" and they were preparing themselves to inherit the earth when God's kingdom on Earth was created. Many other instances can be quoted especially from Matthew which was the one closest in language to the Aramaic.
- Both communities originally cleaved rigidly to the Law of Moses and so, evidently did Jesus because he says in the Sermon on the Mount that he has not come to destroy the Law but to fulfill it and that "one jot or one tittle shall in no wise pass away from the Law till all things be accomplished".
- If the confusion of the timing of the Last Supper in the Bible is anything to go by the calendar used by Jesus did not match the official Jewish one. The Community used a solar rather than the official lunar calendar which might have allowed

113

Jesus and his disciples to have had their Passover meal a day earlier so that he was crucified before Passover started.

- Both communities had an identical ritual meal. The Christian one supposedly specially instituted by Jesus at the last supper, the Community one laid down in the Manual of Discipline in which the priest shall "bless the first fruits of the bread and new wine" after which the Messiah, who is present in spirit, or the Nasi, who is really present, extends his hand over the bread that they might begin.
- Both communities referred to their leader as "Master".
- Both communities held an important gathering at Pentecost.

New Testament scholars believed John was the last of the gospels written and was strongly influenced by Persian religion and Platonic philosophy. From the scrolls however some scholars now take a different view - John follows the tradition of the Essenes.

John has the conflict of Light and Darkness and expressions like, "the light of life", "children of light", "walking in darkness", "the spirit of truth" and "eternal life" all of which occur in the Manual of Discipline. John has:

And all things were made through him, and without him was not anything made that was made.

The Manual of Discipline has the following:

And by his knowledge everything has been brought into being. And everything that is, he established for his purpose; and apart from him nothing is done.

Particularly impressive is the similarity of Matthew 25:35-36 with a passage from the Testament of Joseph. The latter has lines like:

I was beset by hunger and the Lord himself nourished me. I was sick and the Lord visited me. I was alone and G-d comforted me...

While Matthew has:

I was hungry and you gave me food. 1 was sick and you visited me. I was a stranger and you welcomed me...

***

The Essenes lived on the shores of lakes and rivers, away from cities and towns, and practiced a communal way of life, sharing equally in everything. They were mainly agriculturists, having a vast knowledge of crops, soil and climatic conditions which enabled them to grow a great variety of fruits and vegetables in comparatively desert areas and with a minimum of labor.

They had no servants or slaves and were said to have been the first people to condemn slavery both in theory and practice. There were no rich and no poor amongst them, both conditions being considered by them as deviations from the Law. They established their own economic system, based wholly on the Law, and showed that all man's food and material needs can be attained without struggle, through knowledge of the Law.

They spent much time in study both of ancient writings and special branches of learning, such as education, healing and astronomy. They were said to be the heirs of Chaldean and Persian astronomy and Egyptian arts of healing. They were adept in prophecy for which they prepared by prolonged fasting. In the use of plants and herbs for healing man and beast they were likewise proficient.

They lived a simple regular life, rising each day before sunrise to study and commune with the forces of nature, bathing in cold water as a ritual and donning white garments. After their daily labor in the fields and vineyards they partook of their meals in silence, preceding and ending it with prayer. They were entirely vegetarian in their eating and never touched flesh foods nor fermented liquids. Their evenings were devoted to study and communion with the heavenly forces.

Membership in the brotherhood was attainable only after a probationary period of a year and three years of initiatory work, followed by seven more years before being given the full inner teaching.

From its antiquity, its persistence through the ages, it is evident the teaching could not have been the concept of any individual or any people, but is the interpretation, by a succession of great Teachers, of the Law of the universe, the basic Law, eternal and unchanging as the stars in their courses, the same now as two or ten thousand years ago, and as applicable today as then.

The teaching explains the Law, shows how man's deviations from it are the cause of all his troubles, and gives the method by which he can find his way out of his dilemma.

From the Book of Hymns VII of the Dead Sea Scrolls

Thou hast made known unto me Thy deep, mysterious things. All things exist by Thee and there is none beside Thee. By Thy Law Thou hast directed my heart that I set my steps straight forward upon right paths and walk where Thy presence is.

"The Manual Of Discipline" of the Dead Sea Scrolls

The Law was planted to reward the children of Light with healing and abundant peace, with long life, with fruitful seed of everlasting blessings, with eternal joy in immortality of eternal Light.

The Essenes expressed an exceptional knowledge of psychology in their practice of the Communions with the natural and cosmic forces. They knew that man has both a conscious and subconscious mind and were well aware of the powers of each.

In making one group of their Communions the first activity of the morning, they consciously set in motion forces that became the keynote of their whole day. They knew that a thought held strongly enough in the consciousness at the beginning of the day influences the individual throughout his waking hours. The morning Communions consequently opened the mind to harmonious currents which enabled them to absorb specific forms of energy into the physical body.

The evening Communions, performed as the last act in the evening before sleep, applied the same principle. The Essenes knew that these last thoughts influenced the subconscious mind throughout the night, and that the evening Communions therefore put the subconscious into contact with the storehouse of superior cosmic forces. They knew that sleep can thus become a source of deepest knowledge.

Listen to an example of an Essene Communion:

The Angel of Love

Beloved, let us love one another:
For love is of the Heavenly Father:
And every one that loveth is born
Of the Heavenly Father and the Earthly Mother,
And knoweth the Angels.
Ye shall love one another,
As the Heavenly Father hath loved you.
For the Heavenly Father is love:
And he that dwelleth in love
Dwelleth in the Heavenly Father,
And the Heavenly Father in him.
Let him that love him be as the sun
When he forth in his might.
Brothers, be ye all of one mind,
Having endless love and compassion one for another.

They had a profound knowledge of the body as well as of the mind. They knew the two could not be separated as they form a dynamic organic unit, and what affects one affects the other. Essenes antidated psychosomatic medicine by several thousand years.

They paid great attention to the food they ate, that it might harmonize with natural law, but they were equally careful of their diet in thought and emotions. They were fully cognizant that man's subconscious mind is like a sensitized plate registering everything the individual sees or hears, and that it is therefore necessary to prevent all inferior thoughts, such as fear, anxiety, insecurity, hatred, ignorance, egotism and intolerance from entering the gate of the subconscious mind.

The natural law that two things cannot occupy the same space at the same time was clear to them and they knew a person cannot think of two things simultaneously. Therefore if the mind is filled with positive, harmonious thoughts those that are negative and inharmonious cannot lodge in it.

The Essenes believed man should analyze his thoughts and feelings and determine which give him power to carry out a desired action and which paralyze it.

By strengthening all the feelings that create energy and avoiding all those that lead to its exhaustion, the Essenes found that will is acquired. The exercise of will means persevering and patient effort. Through it an individual's superior feelings will gradually create a vast storehouse of energy and harmony; and the inferior feelings, leading to weakness and lack of balance, will eventually be eliminated.

Through their profound understanding of psychological forces the Essene Communions taught man the Way to freedom, the way of liberation from blind acceptance of negative conditions either in the physical body or the mind. They showed the way of optimal evolution of both mind and body.

From "The Book of Hymns" of the Dead Sea scrolls

"I have reached the inner vision

and through Thy spirit in me

I have heard Thy wondrous secret.

Through Thy mystic insight

Thou hast caused a spring

Of knowledge to well up within me,

a fountain of power, pouring forth living waters,

a flood of love and Of all-embracing wisdom

like the splendor of eternal Light."

* * *

INITIATION

When an individual from outside of the order asked to be admitted--and after verification of certain aptitudes for the inner life--the candidate had to practice a kind of meditation. In complete calm, he examined his past life clearly, in order to arrive at an objective summary of it--with the successes, the failures, the motivations, the vibrations experienced, and the wisdom acquired. He had to discern the impulses which he had received from "heaven" and from "his angel" during his childhood and throughout his life, and look at how he had responded. Had he moved away from them, or had he remained faithful?

Through this analysis, a new bond with the higher world of the free spirit could be forged; and the candidate was led to discover his own mistakes--the cause of all of his suffering. In this way, he could bring about changes within himself, take control of his life, and prepare himself effectively, and in full awareness, to enter the Community of Light.

After his initiation, which made him a full-fledged Brother (or Sister) of the community, the newcomer received, simultaneously with his white-linen robe, a mission to be accomplished during his life. This mission had to be a goal, an orientation which must never leave him, and which was a way of uniting him with God and making him useful

119

to the earth and to humanity. He was never to stray from the conducting thread of this mission. This is what gave a positive meaning to his passage on earth and made him a true human being. For the School, to be a man was to carry inside oneself a beautiful light--to be offered to the earth, to its inhabitants and to oneself.

The white robe was a materialization of the power of his baptism and the purity of his soul, which had to protect him from the many contradictions of the world.

The staff, or cane, which he also received on this occasion symbolized his knowledge of the secret laws of life and his ability to use them harmoniously for the successful accomplishment of his task.

He was also required to take an oath to respect the earth as a living, sacred and intelligent being. In order to maintain contact with it, to honor it and to participate in its healthy evolution, he had to be in contact with the ground through his feet--and, sometimes, his whole body. This is why the Essenes were often barefoot.

One had to be at least 21 years old in order to receive this initiation. In order to fulfill this particular mission, the Brother (or Sister) often had to surpass himself, to question himself, and to obtain the assistance of the Holy Spirit.

He was given techniques to help him; for example, he had to examine himself and observe himself often. Every thought, every feeling, every action, and its motivations, had to be clearly outlined "in black and white".

Then, it had to be determined if the idea of the mission, the high ideal, was the source. The Essene Masters knew from experience how quickly one can stray from the path of light and get lost, unable to find the road again.

The necessity to purify oneself constantly--by washing one's feet, hands and body--was very important to the Brothers and Sisters. They cleansed themselves physically and spiritually before entering someone's house, at the beginning and at the end of the day, and before eating or praying. They also washed each other's feet, as a sign of friendship and to cultivate the idea that they must take care of one another, as the Father of all took care of them. They also blessed one another by laying their hands on the top of the head, in order to be always united with the light and to reinforce the love which flowed among them.

* * *

The rules of life, and the very strict discipline which went with them, were not a constraint, but were freely accepted as ways to forge character and to develop in one's highest being.

The Essenes received many teachings of the ancient universal wisdom, which they had to bring to life inside themselves as a sacred service to humanity. They were fully aware that the major part of this wisdom was for a future humanity; and they thought that the great Masters who would come in the future could make use of their work. They believed that, without them--the Masters--the benefactors would not be able to help human beings, and that people would, therefore, sink into the darkness of ignorance and depravity, and eventually destroy one another through wars and other unspeakable atrocities.

The Brothers and Sisters in the white tunic, as they were called then, also practiced a great many humanitarian acts, helping the poor and the outcasts.

The Essenes recognized the equality of the sexes, and accorded to women, in the greatest secrecy, the place which was rightfully theirs. Thus, women were able to participate in all of the spiritual activities.

The technique of Essene initiation consisted in plunging deep inside oneself to find again the source of divine existence which then allowed one to recognize, in the inner level and also around, in the outer level, the living and divine water which animates everything. This water was called the blood of the lamb, the blood of the prophets, of the spiritual Masters, of the great sages of the fraternity and of the people of God.

It is this state of mind, voluntarily cultivated, that opened up the doors of the spiritual worlds to them. Thus, an Essene was conscious of belonging to a people, a tradition, a lineage. It is only when he felt himself in harmony with this lineage that he could really find his place and his fulfillment as an individual amid the community. An Essene could not reach fulfillment outside the lineage of light. Whatever he did in his individual life, had to be linked to the global task. Some cultivated the soil, others were craftsmen, others therapists or teachers… but all of them worked, in one way or another, for the ensemble and the common goal.

From The "Thanksgiving Psalms" of the Dead Sea Scrolls VI

"I am grateful, Heavenly Father,

for Thou hast raised me to an eternal height

and I walk in the wonders of the plain.

"Thou gavest me guidance to reach Thine eternal

company from the depths of the earth.

Thou hast purified my body

to join the army of the angels of the earth

and my spirit to reach

The congregation of the heavenly angels.

"Thou gavest man eternity

to praise at dawn and dusk

Thy works and wonders

In joyful song."

2

THE INNER MEANING OF THE BOOK OF REVELATION

The Greek word apokalypsis (from which we get the English word "apocalypse") literally means "to reveal, to disclose, to uncover...to lift the veil." Prophecy in ancient Israel, even down to the period of the Babylonian exile, had little to do with predicting the future or forecasting historical events. The great prophets of Israel, such as Isaiah or Jeremiah, were primarily concerned with delivering the "word of the Lord," meaning oracles calling on the people to *respond to divine direction*. In other words, apocalyptic literature discloses a transcendent reality. It is meant to influence both the behavior and understanding of the reader by means of divine authority.

In chapter 1 verse 10 of the Revelation, the disciple John tells us that he was "in the spirit on the Lord's day." In this deep state he was caught up in the Spirit of God and "turned" (Rev. 1:12) away from the outer world. He began viewing the inner, heavenly world, and was told to write what he saw and heard. So what John perceived was for his own personal spiritual development as well as for other souls who, by their own development, could sense the true meaning of this story and its strange imagery, and use it to benefit their own journey.

The process John went through to have his revelatory experience, combined with the content of the experience, reveals a spiritual, mystical approach to life. The mystical approach is founded upon a belief that each of us can have an immediate, intuitive perception of spiritual truths that transcend ordinary intellectual understanding by experiencing a direct, intimate union of our soul with God. A way is now opened to experience the Spirit of God and truth directly, not for one or two selected people, but any and all who seek. As Revelation 1:5-6 states it: "...Jesus Christ is the faithful witness, the firstborn of the dead, and the ruler of the kings of the earth. To him who loves us, and released us from our sins by his blood; and he has made us to be a kingdom, to be priests unto his God and Father...." In Jewish tradition, the high priest entered the Holy of Holies and experienced direct contact with God. Now, anyone who asks, will receive; who seeks, will find; who knocks, it will be opened to them (Matthew 7:7 and Luke 11:9).

In order to understand this mysterious, multi-layered text, we must remember that ancient Hebrew (like Greek and other ancient languages) did not have a separate set of characters to indicate numbers, but simply used the letters of its alphabet to represent numbers. This fact provides the basis for the ancient practice of "gematria," in which numerical equivalents of words and names are calculated. Gematria is based on the idea that one may discover hidden meaning in the biblical text from a study of the numerical equivalence of the Hebrew letters. The first letter of the Hebrew alphabet, *aleph* represented one; *beth*, the second letter represented two, and so on.

To understand properly the number systems of the biblical world, one must look to the neighbors of Israel. The Egyptians were already using relatively advanced mathematics by 3000 B.C. The construction of such structures as the pyramids required an understanding of complex mathematics. The Sumerians by that same time had developed their own number system. We still make use of remnants of the Sumerian system today in our understanding of time—12 hours for day and 12 hours for night, 60 minutes and 60 seconds as divisions of time.

In addition to their uses to designate specific numbers or quantities, many numbers in the Bible carried a symbolic meaning. For instance, seven came to symbolize completeness and perfection. God's work of creation was both complete and perfect—and it was completed in seven days.

Israelites were to remember the land and give it a sabbath, permitting it to lie fallow in the seventh year (Leviticus 25:2-7). Major festivals such as Passover and Tabernacles lasted seven days as did wedding festivals (Judges 14:12,Judges 14:17). In Pharaoh's dream, the seven good years followed by seven years of famine (Genesis 41:1-36) represented a complete cycle of plenty and famine.

Multiples of seven had symbolic meaning. The year of Jubilee came after the completion of every forty-nine years. In the year of Jubilee all Jewish bondslaves were released and land which had been sold reverted to its former owner (Leviticus 25:8-55). Another multiple of seven used in the Bible is seventy. Seventy elders are mentioned (Exodus 24:1,Exodus 24:9). Jesus sent out the seventy (Luke 10:1-17). Seventy years is specified as the length of the Exile (Jeremiah 25:12, Jeremiah 29:10; Daniel 9:1: 2). The messianic kingdom was to be inaugurated after a period of seventy weeks of years had passed (Daniel 9:24).

Jesus taught that forgiveness is not to be limited, even to a full number or complete number of instances. We are to forgive, not merely seven times (already a gracious number of forgivenesses), but seventy times seven (limitless forgiveness, beyond keeping count) (Matthew 18:21-22).

The Menorah has 7 candlesticks named Peace, Benevolence, Harmony [or Law?], Light, Truth, Brotherly Love, and Justice.

The seven churches (Revelation 2-3) symbolized by their number all the churches. These represent the seven spiritual centers within the body. In classical Hinduism and Buddhism these centers are called "chakras," which means "wheels," spinning wheels of energy located in specific areas of the human body. Cayce correlates these centers to the endocrine glands, which secrete the powerful hormone messages directly into the bloodstream, affecting all parts of the body. Each of these churches represents a specific spiritual center. The virtue and the fault of each church symbolizes the virtue and fault of that spiritual center within us. These powerful centers affect the soul and mind inhabiting the body. Therefore, the Spirit moves through each church, calling on it to overcome its weaknesses and to do what it knows to do, so that the final glory may be achieved, helping us to prepare for the spiritualization of the mind and heart described in subsequent chapters of the Revelation.

The Seven Lamps of Fire represent the helpful influences that destroy obstacles to the spiritual awakening. These represent the helpful influences that destroy hindrances to the spiritual awakening. They are inner messengers, aids, who stand between the forces of good and evil and become as powers within the nature of man to overcome. This idea may be an extension of the teaching that angels watch over us. An example of this can be found in Psalm 91:11 "For he will give his angels charge over you, to keep you in all your ways." It may also be the power of our inner conscience, that helps us along the way. But with Cayce, it may also be our inner thoughts and chemistry: What thoughts and hormones are we releasing most often? Those that fire up the carnal or violent forces of the body or the gentler, calmer, more uplifting ones, that make the body a temple for the soul?

So the number Seven represents Perfection, the divine number.

After seven, the most significant number for the Bible is twelve. The Sumerians used twelve as one base for their number system. Both the calendar and the signs of the Zodiac reflect this twelve base number system. The tribes of Israel and Jesus' disciples numbered twelve. The importance of the number twelve is evident in the effort *to maintain* that number. When Levi ceased to be counted among the tribes, the Joseph tribes, Ephraim and Manasseh, were counted separately to keep the number twelve intact. In the New Testament, when Judas Iscariot committed suicide, the eleven moved quickly to add another to keep their number at twelve. Twelve seems to have been especially significant in the Book of Revelation. The New Jerusalem had twelve gates; its walls had twelve foundations (Revelation 21:12-14). The tree of life yielded twelve kinds of fruit (Revelation 22:2).

Multiples of twelve are also important. There were twenty-four divisions of priests (1 Chronicles 24:4), and twenty-four elders around the heavenly throne (Revelation 4:4).

An apocryphal tradition holds that seventy-two Jewish scholars, six from each of the twelve tribes, translated the Old Testament into Greek, to give us the version we call today the Septuagint.

Three as a symbolic number often indicated completeness. Prayer was to be lifted at least three times daily.

¹⁶But I call upon God,
  and the LORD will save me.
¹⁷Evening and morning and at noon
  I utter my complaint and moan,
  and he will hear my voice.
¹⁸He will redeem me unharmed
  from the battle that I wage,
  for many are arrayed against me. (Psalm 55: 16-17)

10 Although Daniel knew that the document had been signed, he continued to go to his house, which had windows in its upper room open towards Jerusalem, and to get down on his knees three times a day to pray to his God and praise him, just as he had done previously. (Daniel 6: 10).

The sanctuary had three main parts: vestibule, nave, inner sanctuary (1 Kings 6:1). Three-year-old animals were mature and were, therefore, prized for special sacrifices (1 Samuel 1:24; Genesis 15:9). Jesus said He would be in the grave for three days and three nights (Matthew 12:40), the same time Jonah was in the great fish (Jonah 1:17).

Four was also used as a sacred number. Significant biblical references to four include the four corners of the earth (Isaiah 11:12), the four winds (Jeremiah 49:36), four rivers which flowed out of Eden to water the world (Genesis 2:10-14), and four living creatures surrounding God (Ezekiel 1:1; Revelation 4:6-7). God sent forth the four horsemen of the Apocalypse (Revelation 6:1-8) to bring devastation to the earth. Among the ancients, Four was considered representative of the World of Humanity. For example, there were 4 'elements' (fire, air, earth, water), 4 seasons (spring, summer, fall, winter), 4 eras of human growth (infancy, youth, maturity, old age), and 4 eras of historical growth (gold, silver, bronze, iron).

In the Book of Revelation, we find the Four Beasts. These can be understood as the four fundamental desires of human beings which must be overcome. Revelation's description of each adds to our understanding of these forces and how we may subdue their negative qualities.

The most significant multiple of four is forty, which often represented a large number or a long period of time. Rain flooded the earth for forty days (Genesis 7:12). For forty days Jesus withstood Satan's temptations (Mark 1:13). Forty years represented approximately a generation. Thus all the adults who had rebelled against God at Sinai died during the forty years of the Wilderness Wandering period. By age forty, a person had reached maturity (Exodus 2:11; Acts 7:23).

Ordinary letters were used BOTH as letters and as numbers. The result was that some numbers would spell significant words, and some words had significant numerical values. Gematria was used in the Greek, Hebrew, and Arabic languages. Consider the famous passage from Revelation:

"This calls for wisdom: let anyone with understanding calculate the number of the beast, for it is the number of a person. Its number is six hundred sixty-six." (13:18).

The number Six is a symbol for Imperfection, so it is the number representing humanity. The number 666 in Revelation is often taken as a reverse gematria for the emperor Nero. The name Nero Caesar, put in Hebrew characters and added up total 666. Since "6" represents lack or incompleteness, in contrast to the number "7" representing completion, the triple 666 represents evil.

We can then understand that a term like the Mark of the Beast is a symbol for the unevolved animalistic force within humans

If the meaning of "666" is in the number itself, then the point is clear: The beast is nothing more than human beings under demonic control. In that sense, the "beast" has always been with us, and he can be seen at work throughout the ages.

The Beast is like our ego and egocentric interests. It represents the work of self alone, without God's influence. The mark is erased when the work of our hands and thoughts of our minds are cooperating with God, rather than simply being self-driven. The Beast is our lower nature at our most selfish, self-centered, self-gratifying, self-glorifying point of existence.

The "beast rising out of the sea" is the selfish animalistic desires that arise which are capable of ruling humanity.

In the symbolism of the Apocalypse, such terms as 'death' and 'life' usually refer to 'spiritual death,' etc. ('Leave the dead to bury their dead.'{4}) Death means to be devoid of spiritual awareness and to be without belief in God; sleep means the slumber of heedlessness, to be temporarily devoid of spiritual awareness; life means to have entered the paradise of the love of God.

So the famous reference to Armageddon can be understood to mean the spiritual conflict within humans.

Let's look at some of the other symbolism in Revelation:

[7]Look! He is coming with the clouds; every eye will see him, even those who pierced him; and on his account all the tribes of the earth will wail. So it is to be. Amen. -Rev 1:7

The word 'spiritual' should be associated with the word 'eyes.' This is a reference to the eyes of the mind or heart. To see is to understand.

[16]In his right hand he held seven stars, and from his mouth came a sharp, two-edged sword, and his face was like the sun shining with

full force. When I saw him, I fell at his feet as though dead. But he placed his right hand on me, saying, 'Do not be afraid; I am the first and the last, [18]and the living one. I was dead, and see, I am alive for ever and ever; and I have the keys of Death and of Hades. . -Rev 1:16-18

The right hand is the hand of power and might. As the Spirit of Truth, he speaks with the Sword of Truth, double-edged because it separates the true from the false and the good from the wicked. The sun symbolizes Divinity, the Manifestations of God.

[14]But I have a few things against you: you have some there who hold to the teaching of Balaam, who taught Balak to put a stumbling-block before the people of Israel, so that they would eat food sacrificed to idols. -Rev 2:14-15

'Idol worship' is equivalent to the modern day doctrine of materialism. "To eat things sacrificed to idols" means to believe in (to 'swallow') idolatrous teachings, just as the consuming of the bread and the wine of the Eucharist symbolizes the acceptance of Jesus Christ's teachings and His blood sacrifice.

[4]Yet you have still a few people in Sardis who have not soiled their clothes; they will walk with me, dressed in white, for they are worthy. [5]If you conquer, you will be clothed like them in white robes, and I will not blot your name out of the book of life; I will confess your name before my Father and before his angels. [6]Let anyone who has an ear listen to what the Spirit is saying to the churches. -Rev 3:4-6

Raiment, garment, clothing, etc. mean the character or attributes of the soul. What a person dresses in refers not the literal clothing of the body, but to the clothing of the mind, to mental beliefs and attitudes. All of us are dressed up psychologically in opinions which form mental garments

[9]The great dragon was thrown down, that ancient serpent, who is called the Devil and Satan, the deceiver of the whole world—he was

thrown down to the earth, and his angels were thrown down with him.
Rev. 12: 9

The Great Red Dragon symbolizes that powerful urge within ourselves that originally so separated us from the Source of Life that we fight with those very influences that would bring spiritual awakening. The Great Red Dragon is the serpent from the Garden in Genesis (Rev. 12:9) who first aided in our souls' separation from God's presence.

8 Then another angel, a second, followed, saying, 'Fallen, fallen is Babylon the great! She has made all nations drink of the wine of the wrath of her evil ways. Rev. 14: 8

"Babylon" represents the human desire for earthly riches and success in the gratification of the flesh.

'I know where you are living, where Satan's throne is. Yet you are holding fast to my name, and you did not deny your faith in me* even in the days of Antipas my witness, my faithful one, who was killed among you, where Satan lives. Rev. 2:13

We can understand the reference to the idea of Satan as the force of self-centeredness, self-gratification, self-indulgence, self-importance, self-righteousness, self-consciousness, self-glorification, self-delusion, self-condemnation, self, ego, the "false god," the "beast"

4 And I heard the number of those who were sealed, one hundred and forty-four thousand, sealed out of every tribe of the people of Israel: 5From the tribe of Judah twelve thousand sealed, from the tribe of Reuben twelve thousand, from the tribe of Gad twelve thousand, 6from the tribe of Asher twelve thousand, from the tribe of Naphtali twelve thousand, from the tribe of Manasseh twelve thousand, 7from the tribe of Simeon twelve thousand, from the tribe of Levi twelve thousand, from the tribe of Issachar twelve thousand, 8from the tribe of Zebulun twelve thousand, from the tribe of Joseph

twelve thousand, from the tribe of Benjamin twelve thousand sealed.
Rev. 7: 4-8

The 144,000 is the first group to be sealed and protected from what is coming. Revelation 14 describes them as those who were "redeemed from the earth" (14:4). John says "they have not defiled themselves" (verse 4). The 144,000 follow the Lamb wherever he goes and "no lie was found in their mouths" (verse 5).

The context suggests that the 144,000 symbolize those who are true to God and his way. This group is composed of the spiritually pure, who do not follow false religious and philosophical teachings. They have not refused to repent of ungodly behavior. They are true to God's perfect way.

Those whom God has "sealed" will survive the outpouring of God's wrath. They may suffer trials, persecution or even martyrdom, but they are saved for eternal life.

The sealing of God's servants has much in common with a vision the prophet Ezekiel experienced. He saw human figures in Jerusalem (which is a symbol for the righteous remnant among the tribes of Israel) disturbed over the sins being committed in the city. They also received a "mark" on the forehead, as a sign of their faithfulness to God's way.

Ezekiel 9: 3-4

The LORD called to the man clothed in linen, who had the writing-case at his side, [4]and said to him, 'Go through the city, through Jerusalem, and put a mark on the foreheads of those who sigh and groan over all the abominations that are committed in it.'

To be "sealed" is a symbolic way of saying that the 144,000 are identified as belonging to God. They are "marked" as his special people. In ancient times, a seal commonly indicated possession, much in the way a rancher's brand identifies which cattle belong to him.

Christians can be sure of God's divine care for, "The Lord knows those who are his" (2 Timothy 2:19). The saints are sealed by the Holy Spirit "for the day of redemption" (Ephesians 4:30). Ownership includes protection from condemnation, and the seal of God protects his people. Those who lack this seal face the judgment of God. The plagues fall only on "those people who did not have the seal of God on their foreheads" (9:4).

Revelation's use of numbers also suggests that the 144,000 are not meant as a literal count. Since Israel is a symbol for the church, we should not take the 144,000 as a literal number either. Revelation is a book of cosmic symbols, and, as we have seen, it uses numbers such as seven and twelve in symbolic ways. Twelve is used as a foundational number, such as in the twelve apostles and twelve tribes of Israel. The number 144,000 (12 x 12 x 1000) would then tell us the church is a complete "nation" of large size.

Then I saw a new heaven and a new earth; for the first heaven and the first earth had passed away, and the sea was no more. Rev. 21: 1 Compare this statement with Second Peter 3: 13
[13]But, in accordance with his promise, we wait for new heavens and a new earth, where righteousness is at home.

The New Heaven and New Earth represent a new mind and a new heart. Throughout the Old Testament you may have noticed that the Lord makes occasional reference to giving us new hearts or "circumcising" our hearts.

The "new heaven and new earth" John sees is humanity's perfected state of consciousness and regenerated body. The human mind at this point is now one with the divine in the perfection of control and free from outside limitations.

[12]If you conquer, I will make you a pillar in the temple of my God; you will never go out of it. I will write on you the name of my God, and the name of the city of my God, the new Jerusalem that comes down from my God out of heaven, and my own new name. Rev. 3:12

The number value for New Jerusalem is 1224 which is also the numerical value of the Greek word for "fish". This same number includes "God's creation" "paradise" and "I am the Way". The word Jerusalem means "Sacred Peace".
So the New Jerusalem is the evolved soul in one-ness with divinity.

When humanity recognizes the divinity within them as the controlling force in the world, and turns away from their own selfish pattern of living for self alone, the old pattern disappears and the Christ pattern emerges.

APPENDIX I

THE MOURAVIEFF PHENOMENON

A response to William Patrick Patterson's criticism in his book *"Taking with the Left Hand"* by a student of Boris Mouravieff

Translated from the French by Theodore J. Nottingham

PART ONE

We are in the presence of two texts: --one article (first part) by W.P. Patterson, published in the journal *Telos* under the title "The Mouravieff Phenomenon" and later republished in the book *Taking with the Left Hand*, and which refers to an article by B. Mouravieff published (in the fifties) in the journal *Synthese* before being republished (in the sixties) in the CECE brochure, then translated into English (in the nineties). This article/brochure is titled *"Gurdjieff, Ouspensky and the Fragments of an unknown Teaching"*.

These two texts do not have the same tone: One of them, written by Patterson, is an "emotive expression" while the other, by B.M., is a "teaching". It was destined, among other things, to students (of B.M.) at the University of Geneva.

This difference in tone is also found manifested in the attitudes and methods adopted by each of the authors.

Attitudes and Methods

The judgments and the facts

In his article, B.M. makes a judgment on Gurdjieff, on Ouspensky and on certain disciples of Gurdjieff. This judgment is true or false, just or unjust. But we can see that B.M. was very careful to report a certain number of facts to support his judgment. B.M. did in fact meet Gurdjieff and some of his disciples, he was a friend of Ouspensky's and he brings to us, besides a judgment, a testimonial. Patterson does not have the same scruples. He can bring no testimonial on B.M., having never met him (no more than Gurdjieff or Ouspensky). He bases his judgment on pure hypotheses, pure suppositions, without hesitating to use such phrases as: "He certainly wholeheartedly supported, no doubt encouraged Ouspensky's break...obviously wishing..." "Mouravieff's betrayal would certainly have stunned Ouspensky..."

These unfounded statements take even more direct forms: "Mouravieff's understanding of the teaching could only have been founded on Ouspensky's understanding, not Gurdjieff's..." or "Gurdjieff's mission was to establish the ancient teaching of the Fourth Way in the West as quickly as possible..." or "*Gnosis*, its central ideas lifted directly from Ouspensky's book..."

Patterson fails to bring forth the least fact, the least witness, the least clue, the least element of proof. He only states an opinion, his own, considering it of sufficient weightiness to confuse it with the truth.

The facts and the justification of these facts

Gurdjieff had the power to hypnotize, Mouravieff observed it and Patterson confirms it by reminding us that "before coming to the West, he (Gurdjieff) made his living as a professional hypnotist." This power over people, "this automatic influence over people" bothered Gurdjieff himself and "evoked in him remorse of conscience". Patterson finds the solution: one only needs to justify hypnotism by validating it and considering it an attribute of true "masters". "...we see the same effect with many, if not all, teachers of Gurdjieff's caliber..."

Rather than seeing it as a talent (and a rather disturbing one at that) proper to the man Gurdjieff, a talent which produced "an automatic influence", Patterson exalts this predisposition (with its automatic effects) to the level of advancement on the ladder of consciousness.

In the same way, Gurdjieff's human weaknesses are presented as marks of "courage and love to reveal themselves so unflatteringly". Patterson suggests that Gurdjieff's human weaknesses were intentionally exposed "to keep his students from idolizing him". In this presentation, it is always a matter of justifying and validating the negative.

The last example is given with the evening at baroness de Traubenberg and the famous "two times two". Ouspensky's statement is justified by Patterson's magic wand because it "was completing Mouravieff's assertion" to the son of the baroness "in the sense of asking where in what cases either of the statements is right or wrong, and further, in what instances they might both apply". Who can be fooled by such a obvious distortion: is truth found in one thing, and then in its opposite, and in both at the same time!?!

The facts and their presentation

When Patterson writes: "Mouravieff's negative judgment of Gurdjieff rests on...the perception...Gurdjieff stole the teaching", the statement suggests that this is Mouravieff's perception, a purely subjective assumption leading to a serious accusation: stealing. In fact, B.M. reports the admission from Gurdjieff himself. He brings a testimonial and it is the testimonial of an admission. The minimal space given to this fact can be compared to the long developments which Patterson devotes to his own assumptions. On one side an admission, on the other suppositions. To which does Patterson give more attention?

Analysis of Patterson's attitude

Patterson's attitude reveals a classic psychological process. We can see several aspects of this: The first aspect is evoked by Patterson himself: "the projection onto the teacher". Indeed, it seems that certain individuals cannot approach the Knowledge without associating a name or a face to it. They "personalize" that which, in essence, is beyond all personalizing; and then emotion surpasses thought, that is, intelligence. This is the opposite of the saying "Amicus Plato sed magis amica veritas", and such persons give priority to "amicus Plato" rather than to "amica veritas". They focus their attention on the messenger instead of the message. This personalizing can take the acute form of veneration, not to say idolatry. Then, all questioning of their idol, even in the name of truth, is judged iconoclastic. The "blasphemer" must be punished -- that is, invalidated -- so that the worship of the idol may continue.

The second aspect: he who identifies with the messenger finds himself inevitably wounded by the "attacks" (as they see them) against the idol. His personality, cut to the quick, will react. Pushed on by Nature -- which refuses all suffering -- it will fall back on the "self-tranquilizing machine". We know that, among the means used by the self-tranquilizing machine, there are two primary ones: the first is sentimentality toward oneself, self-pity, the second is accusation of the other. Each of these attitudes -- or both together as they generally form an "infernal couple" -- will calm, place a balm on the wound. And this will occur to the detriment of truth, replaced by justifications and rationalizations calling upon imagination whenever necessary. Not resisting the call of Nature, Patterson used the "accusation of the other" as a reflect to keep the plaster on his idol. Do his accusations bring a response to the heart of the matter which is in question? It is accusation for itself, criticism for itself, not to enlighten a problem but to discredit the adversary as a person.

A third aspect concerns miming mentioned by Patterson elsewhere" "the unconscious miming of the teacher". But the Personality just as unconsciously imitates masters as well as its adversaries. In this accusing reaction, the Personality will rely on accusations that are parallel to those of the offender. This is exactly what is seen in school yards where children say things like: "You are this...,you did that..." and are answered by "No, it's you...!" In the same way, Patterson takes up certain points from Mouravieff regarding Gurdjieff and sends them back to him as in a tennis match.

138

Patterson's subjectivity

When we are "cut to the quick", either we manage to stay and be Present, conscious, or we let Personality react. With the external man, Personality always reacts subjectively.

This subjectivity especially reveals itself in a lack of measure. In the uncentered man, Personality does not know any middle ground and becomes excessive. For example, in this portrait of Ouspensky (whom Patterson never met): "Ouspensky was a rare nature, supremely rational, scientific yet artistic, mystical. Formidable as his intellect was, he was open to feeling and intuition, and so was able..."

This approach is close to being in bad faith, for instance in suggesting that *Gnosis* is "verbiage and lack of clarity and comprehension on the part of Mouravieff". This is proven wrong by many readers who "have commented on the clarity of the text" (preface of *Gnosis II*).

Among the signs of Patterson's subjectivity I would add his tendency to seek out and propose explanations in the social condition of the individuals involved, as if the Being of the individual could be reduced to his social status. He writes (without any proof by the way): "Mouravieff, an exiled aristocrat, had the typical sense of superiority over Russian émigrés he presumed to be socially inferior." "An aristocrat, intellectual and moralist, Mouravieff no doubt had trouble with Gurdjieff's unconventional behavior." It seems that Patterson could not imagine any other criteria to perceive others than through their social circumstances, as if a person could be reduced to a caricature.

Finally, it is surprising that Patterson has such specific judgments without attempting to read B.M.'s other writings (articles, the Stromatas, correspondence with the Groups, the manuscripts in Geneva). Is he worried that reading them might modify his judgment?

Attitudes in the face of duality

The Manifestation is constituted of dualities, opposites: duality of Good and Evil, of affirmation and negation. It is the same for man, the Microcosmos.

If man is conscious, he will observe in himself this duality and feel discomfort. This discomfort, this friction, can -- as Mouravieff explains -- engender a warmth that can start a fire.

In his ordinary state, external man, man asleep, seeks to avoid all tension generated by duality. To this end, he will have a tendency to minimize or eliminate one of the two sides of duality: --either by relativizing the Good, the Truth, affirmation --or by trivializing or legitimizing the Evil, negation --or by inversing their values In this way, he can preserve, nourish and develop his idealizations.

Patterson seems to give only a relative value to Truth: he makes the sentence "two times two never makes four" his own. To suggest the opposite, that "two times two makes four" is considered by him as "absolutism". And absolutism (including the absolutism of Truth) is Evil as opposed to relative Good. And the one who speaks in absolute fashion -- because he transmits Truth -- is treated pejoratively as "one-who-knows".

Patterson also has a great indulgence for Gurdjieff's faults, the "Gurdjieff weaknesses". These are trivialized by the mere fact of their numbers: "he had many as he himself characteristically admits". Moreover, they are legitimized based on the fact that Gurdjieff admits to them. Certainly, the admission of faults is a necessary stage, but it is insufficient to make saints of us!

In the same spirit of legitimizing of the negative, he includes hypnotism, which is transformed to the rank of a quality among the "teachers of Gurdjieff's caliber". Patterson does not specify what that caliber is!

This approach allows Patterson to nourish and preserve his idealizations of Gurdjieff and Ouspensky. That is for him the most important thing. But what to make of the negative? He finds the solution by placing on another all the negative qualities. Thanks to this method, Patterson can perceive only the positive in the idealized person who is painted white (such as his unilateral praising of Ouspensky). On the other hand, we are left with the portrait of Mouravieff, painted in black and unilaterally negative.

PART TWO

The System and Christianity

Patterson criticizes Mouravieff for stripping "Gurdjieff's teaching of its mooring in sacred science and insert it into an Eastern Orthodox Christian perspective..." And he adds peremptorily: "The two teachings simply didn't fit together."

And yet...! Is not the System of Octaves symbolized by the musical scale (tones and semi-tones) as well as by the notes that compose it (Dominus, Sidereus orbis, etc...). Is not the origin of these notes a Christian hymn to John the Baptist? Mouravieff reminds us of this in detail (*Gnosis*, chapter 10). He therefore responds, in preventive measure, to the issues raised by Patterson by showing that Christianity, including its European version, contained the System of Octaves at a certain period.

Going back through Christianity to Judaism, B.M. points out the presence of the System in David's Psalm 118.

Finally, there is no question that the Philokalia contains all the precepts of the Work and its "Christianity" need not be proven...

Besides, Gurdjieff himself -- as B.M. reminds us -- made reference rather often to both monasteries and to Christian esotericism. And, other than questioning B.M.'s witness -- that is, to call him a liar --

Gurdjieff stated to him that the System "was the ABC of Christian doctrine".

By way of appendix, I notice that Patterson's article is illustrated with three "Christian" engravings (Mt. Athos, St. Nicodemus, St. Sophia). Is this an implicit or unconscious recognition?

What is the Fourth Way?

For Patterson, the incompatibility of Gurdjieff's teaching on the Fourth Way and Orthodox Christianity arises from the "mystical and monastic" character of Orthodox Christianity while "the Fourth Way is scientific and rooted in ordinary life."

I see here a double confusion. On one hand, concerning Christianity (Orthodox or otherwise) which certainly can be "mystical and monastic", but can also take other forms. On the other hand, regarding the definition of the Fourth Way, a definition particularly narrow as presented by Patterson. Rather, let us consider Ouspensky's definition (*Fragments*, chapter 2 -- also known as *In Search of the Miraculous* --): "The Fourth Way differs therefore from the others in that it places before man, above all else, the requirement of understanding."

Notice that the distinguishing criteria between this Way and the others certainly does not have to do with an opposition between "scientific" and "mystical", nor between "monastic" and "ordinary life", but that the important criteria which must guide us is "understanding". This understanding is neither scientific nor mystical. Neither reason alone, nor the heart alone can obtain it. It is the precious fruit of conscious work combining the intellectual and emotional centers. And it can be produced among monks as well as among lay people!

Did Mouravieff receive the teaching from Ouspensky?

Mouravieff himself tells us that he learned the System "in 1920-21" in Constantinople through Ouspensky and Gurdjieff. This does not mean that Mouravieff did not follow other teachings, "Christian" teachings for example (see references in the manuscript INITIATION). On this last point, having no information, we can only ask questions: Did Mouravieff have Christian masters? Did they know the System? Or did Mouravieff study for himself "monuments such as the Philokalia", and discovered on his own the keys to the Gospels from Psalm 118?

It would be an exceptional exploit of a self-taught person in a field where everyone claims the importance of an oral tradition. In saying that Ouspensky had "never been initiated in the oral Tradition other than through Gurdjieff", B.M. suggests that he personally had access to this oral Tradition among confirmed masters. But this can only be a deduction, based on our crediting the honesty of Mouravieff; there is no "objective" certainty. Whatever the case may be, we come out of these conjectures with the observation, which is now entirely objective, that *Gnosis* contains more information then *Fragments*. B.M. evaluated the volume of supplementary material in *Gnosis* at one third more than those contained in Ouspensky's *Fragments*. How can Patterson explain that the copier knows more than the one copied, that the thief is richer than the one who is robbed? Certainly, one should analyze the nature of this additional material contained in Gnosis. Are these traditional teachings or ideas belonging to B.M.? It is also possible that Ouspensky, or his inheritors, did not reveal everything in *Fragments*.

But Patterson does not mention the objective fact that Gnosis completes Ouspensky's revelations. Ouspensky's fragmentary message becomes, thanks to B.M., an enlarged message "in the strict limits which are necessary and sufficient to enable the student to go further and in depth through his own creative efforts."

Because of these limits, Mouravieff has not unveiled everything he knows. The necessity of condensing the Knowledge in the three volumes of *Gnosis* was also a break on the expression of what Mouravieff knew and could unveil. The Stromata series (several dozen, perhaps hundreds?) were to complete the omissions and shortcuts found in *Gnosis* due to lack of space.

Gurdjieff's goal

Gurdjieff never clearly announced his goal: "I certainly have a goal...but my goal cannot mean anything to you at this time." What Gurdjieff does not reveal, Patterson miraculously knows and can confide to us: "Gurdjieff's mission was to establish the ancient teaching of the Fourth Way in the West as quickly as possible."

On the other hand, what Patterson does not tell us is by whom was this mission given and in what way Gurdjieff was predisposed to accomplish it. Mouravieff does present certain unfortunate predispositions which are not favorable to the accomplishment of Gurdjieff's supposed mission:

1) Gurdjieff is more the "sorcerer" type (hypnotist) than the teacher in the tradition of Socrates. Considering his type, his teaching activity was in great risk of being contaminated and parasited by the hypnotic influence that he "automatically" exerted over people.

2) According to B.M., Gurdjieff did not possess the intellectual talent to structure and shape the teaching. He had to rely on an intermediary -- Ouspensky. Mouravieff also has reservations on the oral expression which was sometimes brutal and insulting.

This does not mean that Gurdjieff's contribution was entirely negative. On one hand, he "brought his message...without falling into significant contradictions with himself." And we know of the testimonials of others who profited or are profiting from the message and who can "be grateful to the message and its interpreter." But it is also possible, as B.M. points out, that it was those who "could give him resistance" -- that is, persons "sufficiently prepared" -- who truly profited from the message. I was personally taught by such a person. After having met Gurdjieff, she resituated the message, as did B.M., in its Christian context.

The sources of Gurdjieff's teaching

According to Mouravieff, the "work of Gurdjieff" is essentially based on "fragments of the Christian esoteric Tradition". For Patterson, "the two teachings simply didn't fit together".

The divorce is total between these two positions. This divorce does not merely represent a simple disagreement between schools of thought. There are much more important consequences:

1) To isolate Gurdjieff's teaching, to consider it as specific, exclusive of all western reference, is to highlight its "sensational and exotic taste". How many seekers (or pseudo-seekers) are more attracted by the "exotic" than by Truth! To announce "an unknown teaching" can only tickle the natural tendency of amateurs of the sensational to the detriment of a less exalted but more authentic search.

2) Gurdjieff's teaching, limited to himself, is like a potted plant compared to a vegetation that grows in its natural environment. The indefinable richness of vegetation in its proper environment surpasses by far the nature of the isolated and confined plant, however exotic it may be. Gurdjieff's teaching cut off from its natural ground: --certainly reactivated precious keys of understanding that had been forgotten or become hidden --but at the same time impeded the consolidation and blossoming of understanding in its true depth.

For if "the gospel is a book closed by seven locks", it is not the case for the Gurdjieff teaching. For the Gurdjieffian student, this means a progress inevitably limited, if not in fact deviated. And among the many possible deviations we could cite the confusion between the message and the messenger...

Stealing the teaching

Why did Gurdjieff hide his sources? Why does he remain silent on this subject, except in rare exceptional circumstances, such as that encounter with B.M. at the Cafe de la Paix: "I find the system at the foundations of the Christian doctrine. What do you say on this matter? --It is the ABC, he answered me. But they do not understand this!"

Gurdjieff's silence regarding his sources gives birth to a suspicion: he is silent for a reason, because he follows a purely personal goal. This is the very opposite to the accomplishment of a mission. Why would one who fulfills a mission hide his sources?

It is perhaps here that is found the meaning of the phrase "Maybe I stole it...". It could be interpreted as the admission that he was not asked to diffuse this teaching, neither in the East nor in the West. It was a personal initiative on his part, to satisfy a personal interest.

APPENDIX II

An Interview with Ted Nottingham and

The Gurdjieff Internet Guide

GIG: When I first got to know you a bit better I suggested that you might submit some of your articles and reviews to us. All of a sudden you posted a great flow of articles and reviews, although you are fairly busy. Looking at what you are doing can you tell me first on how you find the time to be so productive?

Ted: I have learned over the last quarter of a century of being in the Work that Gurdjieff's concept of "super efforts" is a key aspect of spiritual evolution. This same idea can be found even more vividly expressed in the ancient teachings of Eastern Christianity where the teachers of spiritual awakening developed specific terms such "askesis" (practice), the Russian term "podvig" (daily spiritual struggle), and a host of other methodologies for psychological and spiritual effort in the moment that are fundamental to the process of living each day. In other words, making efforts above and beyond what the natural inclination might be, and done with a specific aim, becomes a regular part of one's life if a search for self-transcendence for the sake of greater meaning is significant.

GIG: It is interesting that you mention 'podvig' and translate it as 'daily spiritual struggle'. Not knowing Russian I have tried to find out the translation for this concept and in the absence of any decided that I might just as well call it 'Conscious Labor and Intentional Suffering'.

I am curious and would like to know what the expression 'ordained minister' means?

Ted: After some years studying the Work, I found the parallels in teachings such as are presented in "The Philokalia" as well as in the writings of the Christian mystics across the centuries. Contemporaries like Thomas Merton also helped to create a bridge into the inner teachings of Christianity, along with the insights of Maurice Nicoll. I pursued my studies by entering a seminary for a masters degree, and was then ordained into a Protestant denomination.
I am now a pastor and spiritual teacher within the framework of a community of faith. For those who understand the technical language of the Fourth Way, this provides exceptional Third Force for one's aims. More importantly, it allows me to live my outer life in conjunction with my inner life. It is a rare privilege.

GIG: Tell me about your contact with the Gurdjieff Work. What brought you to it and did you and do you still take part in it?

Ted: Upon encountering the writings of Gurdjieff and Ouspensky during an intensive period of searching for deeper meaning in life, my life was transformed into a "before and after". After that followed a time of reading all related materials and finding my way into a school where I studied for another four years or so. That was an important experience, yet one that paradoxically proved invaluable because I could "graduate" beyond it. Much could be said about the pitfalls of so-called schools and the limitations of the teachings presented therein. Gurdjieff made it very clear that one had to learn to think for oneself. It is my experience that the existing schools have done to Gurdjieff's teachings what fundamentalism has done to Christianity. I would also remind seekers that the primer "In Search of the Miraculous" was originally titled "Fragments of an Unknown Teaching" for a good reason. I suggest to you that there is a point in the Work that is left "unfinished" or without further elaboration for the very intentional reason that seekers must make the connections and find the next step for themselves.

GIG: I came across the Orthodox Work (as you know it is also called Work) before I learned about Gurdjieff, but it started to make sense only after a contact with the Gurdjieff ideas and a practical study of them. In my view the Gurdjieff Work is a good preparation for the Orthodox Work - the "graduation" you pointed out. However, I know that this "graduation" is just as much possible within the Gurdjieff Work.

I agree that if one takes "The Fragments" to be the Gurdjieff Work then it is incomplete. I am surprised that you consider the Gurdjieff Work to be "unfinished". The group-work, working together in crafts, and taking part in the movements and having his own writings to support the studies, the Gurdjieff Work answers the needs of a person who is interested in self-development, a way to a higher level of consciousness. What is missing?

Ted: There is an entire dimension of Gurdjieff's own life and words that is generally left untouched or unspoken in the presentation of the Teaching. For instance, Gurdjieff said: "You must pray with your whole presence and with all three centers concentrated on the same thing......From realizing the significance of your neighbor when your attention rests on him, that he will die, pity for him and compassion toward him will arise in you, and finally you will love him; also, by doing this constantly, real faith, conscious faith, will arise in some part of you and spread to other parts, and you will have the possibility of knowing real happiness."

These words take us beyond the diagrams, the cosmology, the ribald behavior, to a man of authentic and deep spirituality. There are anecdotes from persons close to him, such as J.G. Bennett, that further confirm this fact: there was a side of Gurdjieff that was not known or shared with his students. This man took care of Russian refugees, assisted the local addict and prostitute in his Paris neighborhood, was related to the Russian Orthodox Church to such an extent that the priest was at his side when he died.

This was a man who valued real faith so greatly that he had no tolerance for superficial piety or social club religion. Therefore, he took an entirely different approach to share the Teaching, one especially suited to early twentieth century agnostics who were in search of something that could not be identified with external religion. In this way, he was able to reach people who would never have made their way into a transforming spirituality. He bypassed old associations made with the ideas of Christ which automatically cut the seeker off from the life-giving teaching behind the words.

I have found this issue of students not understanding the true direction of their teacher's inner life to be true for Karlfried Graf Durckheim. Many of his followers stayed with his early writings dealing with eastern thought and refused to acknowledge that the last ten years of his life -- the apex of his wisdom -- ended up being founded on the spiritual teachings of Orthodox Christianity (particularly the Jesus Prayer) and brought to his work a fullness and completion that was lacking in the early days.

The same is true with Gurdjieff whose nature was profoundly spiritual and rarely understood by his western students who were looking for esoteric lore and self-empowerment rather than genuine transformation leading to humility and goodness. Also, most people of the west know nothing about the form of eastern Christianity that was part of Gurdjieff's world. The break between Rome and Byzantium in 1054 has continued to this day, although these ideas are beginning to surface.

Students who reject any relationship between Fourth Way teachings and spiritual wisdom are generally focused on personal power and elitism. That is a dead end as is clearer demonstrated by the state of being of many such persons.

It must also be said that Gurdjieff was a man of many sides and certainly did not fit into anyone's image of a "holy man". Bennett observed that, at the very end of his life, Gurdjieff's face carried the saddest look he had ever seen. Nevertheless, his contribution is extraordinary and has impacted many lives.

GIG: There are many examples in the different writings of Gurdjieff's relation to Christianity. Before Ouspensky met Gurdjieff Sir Paul Dukes heard him sing The Lord's Prayer and saw the results of his work with a priest in the Alexander Nevsky Lavra on chanting; Dr. Stjörnval thought he was 'Christ himself' etc.. James Moore in his biography asks: '...was Gurdjieff ever tempted to present his teaching explicitly in Christian terms?', but does not pursue the question further. I think you gave an answer to this question when you said that Gurdjieff bypassed old associations by putting the Teaching in a new form. This form works still to-day.

It does sound like you are dissatisfied with the way the Gurdjieff Work is carried on. Are you referring to the secrecy about the Work and that it has been kept to only a few who happen somehow to find it?

Ted: Some self-proclaimed experts on the matter (G.'s infamous "haznamus") have locked the whole system into the events that occurred between 1918 and 1949 and seem obsessed with exploring that bygone era. They have utterly confused the message with the messenger.

It is interesting to note how few of these organizations make use of Maurice Nicoll's brilliant and highly applicable Commentaries which enable students to do real Work on themselves.

GIG: There are many who say they teach Gurdjieff's system or the Fourth Way. I was referring to the only line of the Gurdjieff Work that I have personal experience of. Mine did not have the elements you mention (at least not to an extent that it would have disturbed me). I have met many people who certainly have not been 'crystallized' in the wrong way. Being in their company has given me a 'lift' and these moments are still live and clear in my memory. Nicoll's Commentaries were quoted often by my group leader, Sam Copley, who was a long time student with Nicoll.

To give you one example: I was invited to lunch at Jimmy's, which was a Greek restaurant in an unused underground tunnel in Soho. My friend met me in the company of a young man who was interested in joining the Work. We walked from Piccadilly Circus through the busy streets and had our meal in the noisy restaurant. I can recall details of all this to-day over 30 years later. I lost the thread and went back to sleep after the meal when I walked back on my own and have no recollection of walking to my office in Oxford Street.

This awareness was an influence from a man, who was present, if not all the time, at least most of the time. My friend is now over 70, taking Gurdjieff groups and teaching the movements.

Your experiences of the Work are very different from mine and I am puzzled. This is an important issue for both people who are 'looking for something' and also for people who have found some form of the Work. The different organizations teach the Work based on their understanding and experience of it; some have more some have less. Can you put your finger on this problem?

Ted: I think some of the reasons for our different experiences of people in the Work are the following:
-- I entered some twelve years after you. Already the first generation had died off and was down to a very few.
-- I entered a school which seemed very sophisticated and powerful in regards to the teachings. It is international now in scope, but overshadowed by serious misdeeds of the Teacher. This is where the really dark side came in.
-- I think that in the U.S. it is often easier for organizations and charlatans to turn something into a profit making operation. Also, young Americans are possibly more naive than Europeans and others like yourself and therefore more easily taken advantage of.
-- We are now fifty-two years away from the "sounding of those first notes". This is a different era and a different octave for the Teaching. G. was dealing with 1920's intellectuals. Now the secret teachings of Tibet that he found on his own through colossal effort are in bookstores on sale for less than the price of a sandwich.
Things have turned over several times in human history since then, even since the seventies. Humanity is different. I am not alone in the intuition that the Work cannot exist in a vacuum, disconnected from all other teachings. But it is going to take the ability to leap over great paradoxes and the overcoming formatory mind. This is why there are so few who discover the link between Orthodox Christianity and the Fourth Way. I'm sure there are good people seriously doing the Work now. But there is also degeneration afoot, especially --as you know well -- with the influence of the Internet.

I have found many people to learn from, both in the Work and beyond it; people of joy, light, and deep consciousness, but mostly from the side of mystical religion. The Goettmanns, key students of Durckheim and teachers for many years in their own right in Europe, whose books I have translated, are such examples.
The issue is that, as in all things, the octave has hit an interval and for those who reject the new energy (making

connections), then it can only begin to degenerate. Truth and spiritual evolution, by definition, cannot be the exclusive domain of anyone.

GIG: In a recent interview I asked Dr. Sophia Wellbeloved about some of the ideas that she puts forth in her 'Gurdjieff: The Key Concepts'. One idea that cropped up was if the future of the Work could be making it into a new tradition. If you were in charge how would you like to see the Gurdjieff work to develop?

Ted: There is only one tradition, and that is the evolution into enlightenment which creates people of compassion, maturity, wisdom, and self-transcendence. Every generation must discover the paths that lead to authentic transformation. It isn't about creating new tradition, but about being genuine in one's effort to reach one's highest potential.

GIG: You "graduated" and found contacts that worked for you in the Orthodox circles in France. If you started to look for a teacher, or an elder, where could you think of finding one?

Ted: There comes a time when one no longer seeks for a teacher, but becomes one. The aim is to learn for oneself and become what one is meant to be, not to linger forever at the feet of another person. As for those just beginning the journey, there is only one answer: "Seek and you will find". The intensity of the desire or the yearning will produce results.

GIG: What I know of your own Work is through your homepages and your books. Are you teaching apart from your Ministry and if you do what form it has it taken?

Ted: The form that my teaching has taken now is through the medium of being the pastor of a community. The messages that I share on Sundays are all rooted in practical work on oneself and the effort toward spiritual evolution.

This sharing extends to personal counseling, writing for local newspapers and other media, spending time with people in crisis, and reaching out to seekers whose "magnetic centers" can respond to what they hear from me.

The Work is not for the elite (the word esoteric means inner not secret), but for anyone who has a sincere desire to reach connected with a deeper part of themselves that opens on to encounter with that which is greater than themselves. Emotional healing and purification, self-transcendence, conscious effort, awakening from sleep are the birthright of all who "hunger and thirst" for Truth and right action in the world.

APPENDIX III

Gurdjieff & Orthodox Christianity

By Reijo Oksanen

Introduction

At first look, and even after some study, it is not immediately apparent that the teachings of G. I. Gurdjieff and the Orthodox Startzy or Gerontas are closely related. This is confirmed, often in no uncertain terms, by the followers of both of the teachings. And of course there are not only similarities, but also differences.

Christianity is relative to our understanding of it. Many of the commonly held usual meanings are often wrongly attached to it. To avoid some of these interpretations I want to point out that I am only writing about things like: the following of Christ, of dying to the world and to remember God, and about these and similar things, as they are known in the Orthodox teachings. This study is based on my own studies, in theory and practice, of both the Gurdjieff and the Orthodox Work.

To understand these views it may even be better if you try to forget all what you know about Christianity... unless you have studied the Orthodox tradition and know it well.

The same applies to 'Gurdjieffians'. To me it seems that the 'orthodox' view on the influences that Gurdjieff used in exposing his teaching is that it was predominantly 'Sufic'. I don't know enough to write about these influences, and have not come across anyone who does within the followers of Gurdjieff.

I did say Orthodox Work, because that is what Work is called by both Gurdjieff and the Orthodox (of course other expressions also exist). This is Work on consciousness, indirectly, and finding one's true identity, knowing oneself. The Work is not an end in itself, but a means to reach the aim. Most of it is preparatory Work.

There are similarities and there are differences; I will concentrate on the similarities. The views presented are my own and do not represent the official opinions and attitudes of either of the subjects under study.

My motive in writing is not to try to convince or convert anybody else than myself. To believe in God has always been the great stumbling block in my approach to Christianity. The sermons held by the Lutheran priests that I heard since my childhood have not helped me to understand who God, or the Devil, is. Today, 50 years later, "Who or what is God?" is still for me a big question and a mystery.

If it had not happened that I stumbled into learning about the Orthodox a couple of months before I first read about Gurdjieff I would most likely not have started to find out more about it. This was the reason that led my searches in the direction of the Orthodox teachings, but it does not mean that similar things cannot be discovered in Christianity, whatever the 'Church' one is studying is called.

Most of the Orthodox I have met were born into it. Some of them, but not all, have received the teachings with their mother's milk. God has been a part of their education at home and become a part of their being. I lack this education and it justifies my search and this study.

This is quite different with the Gurdjieffians - by far the majority of them came across the teachings at a later time in their lives.

Monasticism & the Fourth Way

Gurdjieff: "There is not and there cannot be any choice of the people who come into touch with the 'ways'. In other words, nobody selects them, they select themselves, partly by accident and partly by having a certain hunger." [Ref. 1]

The Orthodox say that the Christian life is the same for everyone independent of where one lives. 'Dying' to the world and 'remembering God' continuously are such hard labours that some people choose to follow the way to the union with God without the distractions of the daily life in the 'worldly' occupations. Withdrawing to a monastery or a convent does not change any of the difficulties or make this work easier; the novices carry the sins of their souls (and their thoughts and emotions) and of their bodies wherever they go.

Our energy is limited and used up in many ways. We 'leak' our energy through our functions: thoughts, feelings and sensations. This is all part of human nature, 'old Adam and Eve'. The 'sins of the soul' and the body can only be purified by the Lord sitting on his throne. A Christian struggles to beat this 'legion' and to prepare the way for the 'Spirit', the Lord. Gurdjieff expresses a similar struggle by saying that as we are, we have no 'real I', no Master, but a multitude of petty little I's. To be a Master is the aim.

Lord on His throne to me looks the same as having the Master in our house; he sees our faults, does not condemn, but forgives. Repentance (Greek word metanoia means turning one´s direction) is an Orthodox minute to minute activity, which is only possible when our Conscience is not 'buried' (Gurdjieff). We need to see our nothingness or as Gurdjieff puts it, "we cannot enter heaven with our boots on" or "eating cakes".

Going to reclusion can be seen as an attempt to lessen the impact of the world and coming into a situation where one is reminded all the time of 'the only thing necessary' - the remembrance of God and the union with Him. Bishop Alexander Miloant wrote: "Orthodox monasticism has always been associated with stillness or silence, which is seen primarily as an internal rather than an external state. External silence is sought in order to attain inner stillness of mind more easily".

Gurdjieff says in P. D. Ouspensky's book In Search of the Miraculous: "You must understand that every real religion, that is, one that has been created by learned people for a definite aim, consists of two parts. One part teaches what is to be done. This part becomes common knowledge and in the course of time is distorted and departs from the original. The other part teaches how to do what the first part teaches. This part is preserved in secret in special schools and with its help it is always possible to rectify what has been distorted in the first part or to restore what has been forgotten. Out of dozens of monasteries one is a school." [Ref. 2]

Gurdjieff used the expression the Fourth Way to distinguish his teachings from other Ways. To me it looks that the expression Fourth Way was a 'sales trick'. It was mainly used in the early days of the teaching and adopted by P. D. Ouspensky when he taught what he called the 'system' quite independently of Gurdjieff, but based on the ideas he had learned from him.

The Fourth Way is practised in life by those who do not have a possibility to give up everything and go to a monastery. In Christianity this is the practice of the lay people. In fact the conditions the seeker of truth finds himself when coming in contact with the Fourth Way are ideal for his/her work. [Ref. 3]

I detect a certain self-satisfaction when Gurdjieff says that he has 50 sons in monasteries. It is my opinion that the concept 'Fourth Way' is very unfortunate and misleading. It seems to imply that outside the traditional ways of the Fakir, Monk and the Yogi, there are no possibilities of finding a Way, apart from his Fourth Way. I do not think that this is what Gurdjieff really wanted to say, or actually said.

To put it in Christian words: the Fourth Way is only for *lay people*, because there is no Fourth Way monasticism. Christianity has also been always open for the lay people.

Here lies another similarity: both teachings need to be found. They only become available with dissatisfaction with my own life as it is and through a search for an entirely new approach to it.

The World's Best Kept Secret

Gurdjieff: "Thus the work of collecting scattered matter of knowledge frequently coincides with the beginning of the destruction and fall of cultures and civilizations". [Ref. 4]

Orthodox Christianity has been called "The World's Best Kept Secret". The main reasons for this is language in many different aspects. The writings have been available for many hundreds of years in different languages like Syrian, Greek and Russian. Only in the latter part of the 20th century a larger selection of this literature has been translated into English. Some of these translations were made by E. Kadloubovsky and G. E. H. Palmer (two works published in the early fifties and one in 1966 [Ref 5,6,7]), who both had their association with P. D. Ouspensky as his students. Ouspensky writes: "G. Many times pointed out the necessity of studying this forgotten 'technique' as well as the impossibility of attaining results of any kind on the way of religion without it, excepting purely subjective results." [Ref. 8]

161

Another 'language difficulty' is that it is hardly possible to approach a spiritual father, a staretz or Geronta, for instructions if you do not speak his language. Yet another reason for the difficulty is a direct result of the forms Christianity has taken in the West - the Eastern teachings are so different, that a considerable openness is necessary on the part of a Western person to understand what the Eastern mystics said and thought. The language and the expressions used are the main difficulties.

It is at this point Gurdjieff with his vision and with the clear language he used comes to help. His language is direct and it is not often even lost in the translation. This applies both to theory and practice. In other words he comes up with some keys that can open some of the doors to "The World's Best Kept Secret." This works both ways - some keys to Gurdjieff's teaching can be found in the Orthodox theory and practice; these teachings are complimentary to each other.

Below are two samples of this use of language, which also show the difference of the use of expressions and how they are complimentary:

Theophan the Recluse writes *in The Path to Salvation*: "*I am a Christian,* you say, and content yourself with this. This is the first deceit - transferring to yourself the privileges and promise of Christianity, without any care to root true Christianity into yourself; or to ascribe to yourself that which can only be acquired by your strength and inner worthiness." [Ref. 9]

The above is clear enough. Gurdjieff says *in P. D. Ouspensky's In Search of the Miraculous*: "First of all it is necessary to understand that a Christian is not a man who calls himself a Christian or whom others call a Christian. A Christian is one who lives in accordance with Christ's precepts. Such as we are we cannot be Christians." [Ref. 10]

Orthodox Monasticism has jealously guarded their communities against the sinful influences coming from the 'World', particularly influences from the West. This clash has always been there, but a definite opening in Russia towards the rest of the World has at least and at last become possible after the fall of the Soviet rule. However, the outside influences need to be kept at bay simply to maintain the special conditions in the Monasteries.

This guarding from the sinful influences has also extended to the influences with the Orthodox monasticism itself. When the monks started to practice the 'Prayer of the Heart' it was condemned by the Church authorities and those who practiced it were called 'naval gazers'. Later in the 15th century the Prayer of the Heart was though accepted and those who were against it were kicked out of the church.

It took a hundred years for the Orthodox to accept some of the main writings of Theophan the Recluse (1815–1894), who was made a Saint in 1980.

Gurdjieff's teaching is in the same situation to-day and far too 'unorthodox' to be accepted by the Orthodox authorities.

Gurdjieff: Man Can Not Do;

Jesus: For without me you can do nothing (John: 15).

Gurdjieff: "Man's chief delusion is his conviction that he can *do*. All people think that they can do, all people want to do, and the first question all people ask is what they are to do. But actually nobody does anything and nobody can do anything. This is the first thing that must be understood. *Everything happens.*" [Ref. 11]

163

The Orthodox say that thoughts, which are good or bad, lead to emotions (the strong ones are called passions), also good or bad, and the emotions lead to actions, which again are good or bad. Work consists in knowing one's self, seeing all these movements, both the good and the bad ones.

St. Theophan the Recluse: "The result of warfare can be a mind free of thoughts, a heart free of passions, and a will free of tendencies. When this develops, the person has achieved passionlessness. His inner being becomes a clear mirror that reflects spiritual things." [Ref. 12] The method to achieve this is doing the opposite of what our 'old Adam or Eve' does. 'The Law of the Opposites' is also part of the Gurdjieff-teachings.

About Self-Remembering and Self-Gathering

St. Theophan: "Gathering is where all spiritual work takes place - warfare, reading, divine contemplation and prayer. Whatever the ascetic does, he should always go within and work from there". [Ref. 13]

Gurdjieff defines self-consciousness as the third state of consciousness, with sleep and waking-sleep (our normal state) as the two lower states. The way to self-consciousness is through the practice of self-remembering, by dividing attention between my sense of 'I' and an object. The object can be within me or outside me. This has an effect in Gurdjieff's words: "everything more vivid". I do not normally remember myself and to do it I need to make an effort, every time - it does not become automatic. The exercise to do this was described on the Gurdjieff Internet Guide site in detail in an article by A. G. E. Blake and is now available at http://www.katinkahesselink.net/sufi/foundations.html

Self-gathering is the Orthodox preparatory work. There are three
164

elements in self-gathering. First: the gathering of the mind in the heart, called attention. Second: to be alert in the body, called vigilance. Third: to come to the senses, called soberness. To be self-gathered you descend within your heart with the help of these three elements. When you are within the work is to remain there as long as you are conscious. When you are outside, your repeat the self-gathering and go on renewing it as it is not something that continues without the effort. When you have gathered yourself, you are within; missing even one of the elements puts you outside. In fact St. Theophan writes: "...the ascetic laborer is in a minute-by-minute struggle...Therefore he is in a state of perpetual beginning..." [Ref. 14]

For Gurdjieff work and the Orthodox work self-remembering and self-gathering are the methods that make further work possible. They are the preparatory works that can lead to the death of the tyrant that keeps the 'real I', 'the Spirit', in prison. The death of this tyrant (old Adam and Eve) can eventually make new birth, the birth of "I", the birth of Christ, possible.

Prayer

Full and real prayer is when praying words and praying thoughts are combined with praying feelings. [Ref. 14A]

Gurdjieff had his way of expressing what prayer is. To answer a question if prayer can help in the work and how one can pray he said: "You can only pray with your three centres, and at the same time it is an exercise. What interests me is not your prayer, it is your concentration with your three centres. Your prayer goes no further than your atmosphere... Learn, for the sake of the future, to concentrate not only with one center but with the three. You must think, feel and sense. This is important. For this there are different

165

exercises. You can pray, sing - anything you like - but with the three centers." [Ref. 14B]

St. Theophan: "First prepare yourself: 'stand for a while in silence, until your feelings calm down' as the prayer-book teaches, and remember what you are about to approach and to perform, who you are, who are about to pray, and who is He before Whom you are about to recite your prayers, what exactly you are to say and how." [Ref. 14C]

Soul

St. Theophan: All of these activities are assigned for the development of the powers of the soul in the spirit of a new life. [Ref. 15]

Soul is an interesting word. It is used in Orthodoxy of thoughts and emotions, of our 'ordinary' thoughts and emotions. We have this ordinary soul and a body. These are not perfect as they are, but give us the possibility of work, the material. This 'soul' has to die for 'Christ' to be born in us. When the Spirit, Christ, is present, our soul is in connection with Him and through this connection our souls can be purified. We are not born with the Spirit, but according to Christianity, it enters us when we are baptized. We are not aware of it (at least most of us are not) and if we do not wake up to the presence of the Spirit the soul remains impure.

Gurdjieff says that as we are we have no soul. According to him we have fully developed 'higher centers', which we are only very rarely in touch with (we are not aware of their workings). To have a soul we first have to make it.

The main reason for the 'lack of soul' and our 'soul's impurity'

(Orthodox) is that our education is wrongly conducted. This is very difficult to rectify in later life. However, we can awake, and the soul can become alive and purified in us through remorse of Conscience.

Conscience & Morality

Beelzebub: "...although the factors for engendering in their presences the sacred being-impulses of Faith, Hope and Love are already quite degenerated in the beings of this planet, nevertheless, the factor which ought to engender that being-impulse on which the whole psyche of beings of a three-brained system is in general based, and which impulse exists under the name of Objective-Conscience, is not yet atrophied in them, but remains in their presences almost in its primordial state". [Ref. 16]

Gurdjieff differentiated between subjective and objective morality. Subjective morality is artificial and different in China and Europe. It is also different within the classes in a society. The more moral you are the more immoral other people seem to be.

The aim of Orthodox morality is to attain union with God; it deals with man's relationship to God. Man is by nature weak and lacks quality. In fact his being determines his God.

Orthodox morality is conscious and voluntary doing of God's will. Its opposite is slavery - man's reasoning, habits, external influences, education etc. Freedom is choosing between the egoistic will and the will of God.

I made the following translation from a 100 page book by a Finnish Orthodox priest published in 1947 about Conscience:

"The criticism of man's actions take place in his conscience; its influence does not
167

extend outside himself. The criticism in his conscience must be preceded by actions done consciously and voluntarily. Only this makes man responsible for his actions, words, and thoughts; also those of other people if he has influenced them."

"A wish is a moral feeling that draws man towards perfection. This wish is only influenced by conscious and voluntary efforts. After numerous efforts man can arrive at creating rules for himself. This he can do with the help of self-observation and logical reasoning. These rules are always common for all people, always the same and always necessary. There can be no development in them."

"When man understands that this objective moral law is meant personally for him, he also understands his duty. Man has only one duty, but it can contain different activities. He must have a clear picture of the order of importance and urgency of these actions in relation to his duty as otherwise he gets confused."

"Conscience keeps man informed of his moral law (rule). Conscience is of two kinds: law-giving and critical. The law-giving conscience says what man has to do; the critical conscience in him judges how he has done it. Conscience can develop, become more responsive and more perfect."

Gurdjieff: "*Conscience* is a state in which a man *feels all at once* everything that he in general feels, or can feel." [Ref. 17]

"Even a momentary awakening of conscience in a man who has thousands of different I's is bound to involve suffering. And if these moments of conscience become longer and if a man does not fear them but on the contrary co-operates with them and tries to keep and prolong them, an element of very subtle joy, a foretaste of the future 'clear consciousness' will gradually enter these moments." [Ref. 17A]

The Quest for Freedom and Obedience

St. Theophan: "...the renunciation of our own freedom. A free creature, according to his consciousness and determination, acts from his own self, but this should not be so. In the kingdom of God there should not be anyone acting from himself; God should be acting in everything. This cannot happen as long as freedom stands for itself - it denies and turn away God's power". [Ref. 18]

It is said in the Gurdjieff work that at some point we have to come under the will of another, someone, who we trust, 'a teacher', even if we do not always agree. In the absence of a 'teacher' God is available for this, all the time. The problem is that we are not always present, we are 'upside down'. Monasteries provide the opportunity to come under another will, the Will of God and that of the Spiritual Father, the Staretz. This opportunity is also open to lay people if they find a contact with 'one who knows'.

There has to be a 'guide', be that an elder, Staretz, Geronta or in the Gurdjieff work a group and a leader who is awake and can keep shaking us as long as it takes to get us 'to blink' and eventually to wake up. Learning can take place when we obey!
In other words both of these teachings are oral teachings; direct advice from the guide to the guided. Without the direct contact we go our own way and it often happens that we lose it.

What about my freedom then?

Gurdjieff in Ouspensky's In Search says: "The whole thing is in being ready to sacrifice one's freedom. A man consciously and unconsciously struggles for freedom as he imagines it and this, more than anything else, prevents him from attaining real freedom. But a man who is capable of attaining anything comes sooner or later to the conclusion that his freedom is illusion and he agrees to sacrifice this illusion. He voluntarily becomes a slave. He does what he is told, says what he is told, and thinks what he is told. He is not afraid of losing anything because he knows that he has nothing. And in this way he acquires everything. Everything in him that was real in his understanding, in his sympathies, tastes, and desires, all comes back to him accompanied by new things which he did not have and could not have had before, together with a feeling of unity and will within him. But to arrive at this point, a man must pass through the hard way of slavery and obedience. And if he wants results he must obey not only outwardly but inwardly. This requires a great determination, and determination requires a great understanding of the fact that there is no other way, that a man can do nothing himself, but that at the same time, something has to be done." [Ref. 19]

On my first visit to Mount Athos in 2010, I had the opportunity to ask from a monk how they practice the Prayer of Jesus. He answered: "It may be sounding a bit strange to you, but our practice is through Obedience".

Suffering

Gurdjieff: "If you try to do something you don't want to do - you will suffer. If you want to do something and don't do it - you also suffer". [Ref. 19A]

In Gurdjieff Work, Intentional Suffering is one of the two principal ways to Work on oneself (the other is Conscious Labour). He says that most of the time we suffer because of our corns, which is not worth 'one Franc'. With Intentional Suffering we help Our Common Father Endlessness and alleviate his sorrow. [See Beelzebub's Tales]

Doing the opposite and opposing the demands of the body and the soul (thoughts and emotions) are the beginning of asceticism. This struggle of man with himself is called in Russian *podvig* and used by the Orthodox to depict the pain and the hard Work, the unseen warfare.

The need for a guide is essential for this Work. St. Theophan the Recluse writes: "Whoever conducts warfare with himself is conducting it *himself*, and while trying to work against egotism he is in a way feeding it. With a guide our "I" and its will entirely disappear at the outset, and together with it the passions lose all support." [Ref. 20]

All the sorrows and unpleasantness that an Orthodox meets are sent from God as a gift to give material for this Work of uprooting the passions (meaning strong emotions).

Centers & Brains - Aspects & Degrees

Gurdjieff: "Man is a three-brained being".

There is an interesting passage in St. Theophan's 'The Spiritual Life', which is directly related to Gurdjieff's concept of brains and centers. He calls them 'aspects', 'degrees' and 'layers':

"There are five layers in all, but one person in man, and this one person lives first one life, then another, then a third life. Judging by this, a person receives a particular character according to the kind of life he lives, and this character is reflected in his views and attitudes, his habits, and his feelings. That is, his life is either spiritual, with spiritual views, habits and feelings; or it is intellectual, with intellectual concepts, habits and feelings; or it is carnal, with carnal thoughts, deeds and feelings. (I am not taking into consideration the states in between - the intellectual-spiritual, or the intellectual-physical, because I don't want too many categories). This does not mean that when a man is spiritual that the intellectual and physical

171

have no place in him, but only that the spiritual predominates, subordinating to itself and penetrating the intellectual and the physical parts." [Ref. 21]

On the same page he continues: "Man is always free. Freedom is given to him along with consciousness of self, and together they constitute the essence of the spirit and the standard of humanity. Extinguish freedom and consciousness of self, and you extinguish the spirit, and man is no longer man." [Ref. 21]

In Gurdjieff's teachings 'The Harmonious Development of Man' is possible with 'self-remembering' and a man who remembers himself is self-conscious. Although the language is somewhat different both are speaking of the same things, which becomes apparent when St. Theophan writes:

"...spirituality is the norm of human life, and so as a result, being spiritual, he is a real person, whereas the intellectual or carnal man is not a real person." [Ref. 22]

It looks to me that Gurdjieff clarified these concepts. For St. Theophan living without a Spirit brings us into a whirlpool of thoughts, emotions and actions "sometimes for a short time, sometimes for a long time, and not infrequently forever." [Ref. 22] He goes on to say that this turbulence is abnormal and an illness, but it can be healed.

St. Theophan writes of the Spirit, intellect and body (carnal man). Why does he not mention 'the emotional man'? The heart for the Orthodox (and many others) is the seat of emotions, not in the sense of the physical muscle, but more as occupying that part of the human body. His view on the emotions is what is said about the passions; they are not what they should be and if they are not uprooted they

172

are the biggest obstacle in our Union with God. Self-consciousness and freedom are only possible when the passions don't rule.

The Gurdjieff-approach to this was well defined by Adam Nott in the 2003 All & Everything Conference (I have edited this from the Proceedings, because the original is rendered in such a way that it can hardly be understood):

"What is the difficulty about seeing ourselves?

The most obvious difficulty is that at the moment when one glimpses some aspect of oneself, which one could learn from, there is a reaction; one can be either pleased or disappointed. I am usually disappointed or shocked at the behaviour that I see and then I am taken by the reaction and what I have seen does not leave an impression.

The question becomes: *'How is it possible to see and not react?*

This is only possible when the centres are connected. The level of reaction is a level where one centre has dominated. In order to see it is necessary for the centres to be connected.

How is this possible? This brings us to the fundamental question.

How is it possible for the centres to be connected?

Before three centres can be connected, two need to be connected. Which two? If I try to connect my emotions with my body or with my mind the emotions are so strong that there is no possibility of a relationship. If I try to connect my body to my head there is a possibility of a relationship. If that relationship can be maintained the feelings can come in.

173

How do I connect my body with my head?" [Ref. 22A]

Adam Nott goes further by saying that this is a discovery that one has to make. I wish to add that the exercise given in the above link by A. G. E. Blake in his article and the practice of the Prayer of the Heart are both about this discovery.

Some Conclusions

Gurdjieff left Russia in 1920 when the communist regime had begun the destruction of religion and the religious people. Many of the monks and nuns were killed (the statistics of this say that 88000 monks, nuns and priests were killed). The monasteries, convents and churches were used for the purposes of communism in the Soviet area. When I visited St. Petersburg (then called Leningrad) in the seventies and wanted to see the Theological Academy near Alexander Nevsky Monastery, the buildings were used for weapon production and access was denied.

By the time Gurdjieff arrived in the West with his teaching the whole of the Orthodox tradition of the Elders in Soviet Union had to go underground. Only a few traces of it are left now after the Soviet fall. Today it is in the process of being built up again. The work of the Gerontas in Mount Athos could continue through this time, and has been under renewal from the seventies.

In the Gurdjieff related literature there are some references saying that Gurdjieff stole the ideas from somewhere - he started these rumours himself. When asked where he got his knowledge, he once answered: "Perhaps I stole it". He certainly was inspired by the Orthodox inner teachings. He put them in a form that is more accessible in our time. However, stealing in this area is not possible, as it is a question of being and being present.

Gurdjieff: "No, we are a group of friends. About 30 years ago a dozen of us spent several years in central Asia, and we reconstructed the doctrine from the remains of oral traditions, from the study of ancient customs, folk songs and even from certain books. The doctrine has always existed, but the tradition has often been interrupted. In ancient times certain groups and castes knew it, but it was incomplete. The ancients went in too much for metaphysics. The doctrine was too abstract." [Ref. 22]

Gurdjieff said towards the end of his life: "Remember what now I say, begin in Russia, finish in Russia". Why did he say that? He had kept the Orthodox tradition similar to the teachings of the elders alive with his teaching. Did he want to go back and hand it over to the church?

James Moore writes in his website http://www.gurdjieff.org.uk/gs9.htm that it is possible that in 1935 Gurdjieff applied for permission to return to Russia and went on a journey for about three months the same year, perhaps visiting also Leningrad.

It is not surprising, although there is perhaps no way to verify the truth of what Ted Nottingham writes about in his review on Robin Amis' book "A Different Christianity" at http://www.gurdjieff-internet.com/book_details.php?authID=28&BID=126&lang=Englis h: "In a striking anecdote resulting from his years of research, Amis informs us that, shortly before his death, Gurdjieff arranged for a group to travel to Mount Athos in an effort to re-establish contact with the tradition. The author claims that making the connection with this ancient teaching virtually lost to the world completes the incomplete system of inner work which Ouspensky called "fragments of an unknown teaching."

Before Gurdjieff's 'literary ambassador' P. D. Ouspensky died, he 'abandoned the system' he had been teaching for nearly 30 years. His advice to his followers was to 'reconstruct the system'. As far as I know no re-construction has taken place.

I do not think that Gurdjieff's teaching is incomplete, neither is the Orthodox inner tradition. It has been of benefit for me to study both. Perhaps some day some others will also find this study beneficial (like some already have) in their attempts to Work; irrespective of if they call themselves 'Gurdjieffians' or 'Orthodox Christians', or both.

References:

[Ref. 1] P. D. Ouspensky: In Search Of The Miraculous(Search). London: Routledge & Kegan Paul, 1957; page 360

[Ref. 2] Search, p.38

[Ref. 3] Search, p. 304

[Ref. 4] Search, p. 48

[Ref. 5] Anonymous: Writings from the Philokalia on Prayer of the Heart (Philokalia, Heart). London: Faber & Faber, first published in 1951

[Ref. 6] St. Theophan the Recluse: Unseen Warfare (Warfare). London: Faber & Faber, first published in 1952

[Ref. 7] Igumen Hariton: The Art of Prayer (Art). London: Faber & Faber, 1966

[Ref. 8] Search, p. 304

[Ref. 9] St. Theophan the Recluse: The Path to Salvation (Path). U.S.A.: St. Herman of Alaska Brotherhood, 1996, p. 133

[Ref. 10] Search, p. 102

[Ref. 11] Search, p. 21

[Ref. 12] Path, p. 302

Ref. 13] Path, p. 226

[Ref. 14] Path, p. 217

[Ref. 14A] Warfare, p. 205

[Ref. 14B] Meeting Transcripts, 1941

[Ref. 14C] Warfare, p. 208

[Ref. 15] Path, p. 260

[Ref. 16] Gurdjieff: All & Everything. London: Routledge & Kegan Paul, 1950, p. 359

[Ref. 17] Search, p. 155

[Ref. 17A] Search, p. 156

[Ref. 18] Path, p. 316

[Ref. 19] Search, p. 365

[Ref. 19A] Gurdjieff: Views from the Real World, London, Routledge & Kegan Paul, 1973, p. 101

[Ref. 20] Path, p. 306

[Ref. 21] St. Theophan: The Spiritual Life (Spiritual). U.S.A.: St. Herman of Alaska Brotherhood, 1995, p. 71-72

[Ref. 22] Spiritual, p. 74-75

[Ref. 22A] The Proceedings, All & Everything Conference, 2003, p. 128

[Ref. 23] Denis Saurat: 'A Visit to Gourdyev', The Living Age, New York, January 1934, Vol. CCCXLV (4408), pp. 427–433

Printed in Great Britain
by Amazon ·

79787262R00108